W9-BKU-211

Debates on the Crusades

Don Nardo

San Diego, CA

Printed in the United States

For more information, contact:
ReferencePoint Press, Inc.
PO Box 27779
San Diego, CA 92198
www. ReferencePointPress.com

LIBRARY OF CONGRESS CATALOGING-IN-PUBLICATION DATA

Names: Nardo, Don, 1947– author.
Title: Debates on the Crusades/by Don Nardo.
Description: San Diego, CA: ReferencePoint Press, Inc., [2019] | Series: Debating History | Includes bibliographical references and index. | Audience: Grades 9–12.
Identifiers: LCCN 2017059609 (print) | LCCN 2018016065 (ebook) | ISBN 9781682823668 (eBook) | ISBN 9781682823651 (hardback)
Subjects: LCSH: Crusades—Juvenile literature.
Classification: LCC D157 (ebook) | LCC D157 .N37 2019 (print) | DDC 909.07—dc23
LC record available at https://lccn.loc.gov/2017059609

Contents

Foreword

Is slavery immoral?

No thinking person today would argue that slavery is moral. Yet in the United States in the early and mid-1800s, slavery was an accepted institution in the southern states. While many southerners never owned slaves, the institution of slavery had widespread support from plantation owners, elected officials, and even the general populace. Its defenders were often respected members of their communities. For instance, John C. Calhoun—a US senator from South Carolina—was a staunch defender of slavery. He believed that enslaved Africans benefited from their status as slaves—and said as much during an 1837 Senate speech. "Never before," he stated, "has the black race of Central Africa, from the dawn of history to the present day, attained a condition so civilized and so improved, not only physically, but morally and intellectually."

Statements like this might be confounding and hurtful today. But a true understanding of history—especially of those events that have altered daily life and human communities—requires students to become familiar with the thoughts, attitudes, and beliefs of the people who lived these events. Only by examining various perspectives will students truly understand the past and be able to make sound judgments about the future.

This is the goal of the *Debating History* series. Through a narrative-driven, pro/con format, the series introduces students to some of the complex issues that have dominated public discourse over the decades—topics such as the slave trade, twentieth-century immigration, the Soviet Union's collapse, and the rise of Islamist extremism. All chapters revolve around a single, pointed question, such as the following:

- Is slavery immoral?
- Do immigrants threaten American culture and values?
- Did the arms race cause the Soviet Union's collapse?
- Does poverty cause Islamist extremism?

This inquiry-based approach to history introduces student researchers to core issues and concerns on a given topic. Each chapter includes one part that argues the affirmative and one part that argues the negative—all written by a single author. With the single-author format, the predominant arguments for and against an issue can be synthesized into clear, accessible discussions supported by details and evidence, including relevant facts, quotes, and examples. All volumes include focus questions to guide students as they read each pro/con discussion, a visual chronology, and a list of sources for conducting further research.

This approach reflects the guiding principles set out in the College, Career, and Civic Life (C3) Framework for Social Studies State Standards developed by the National Council for the Social Studies. "History is interpretive," the framework's authors write. "Even if they are eyewitnesses, people construct different accounts of the same event, which are shaped by their perspectives—their ideas, attitudes, and beliefs. Historical understanding requires recognizing this multiplicity of points of view in the past. . . . It also requires recognizing that perspectives change over time, so that historical understanding requires developing a sense of empathy with people in the past whose perspectives might be very different from those of today." The *Debating History* series supports these goals by providing a solid introduction to the study of pro/con issues in history.

Important Events of the Crusades

1095
Pope Urban II urges Christians from across Europe to travel eastward and wrest control of Jerusalem and the rest of the Holy Land from the Turks.

1098
The first crusader state is established at Edessa (now eastern Turkey).

1099
Jerusalem falls to the crusaders, most of whom then return to their homes in Europe.

1096 1097 1098 1099 1100 / 1140

1144
Zengi, Muslim ruler of Mosul, captures the crusader state of Edessa, causing widespread concern in Europe.

1146
In response to the fall of Edessa, Pope Eugenius III calls on the faithful to join the Second Crusade.

1096
Tens of thousands of European Christians begin to answer the pope's call for a holy war, known as the First Crusade.

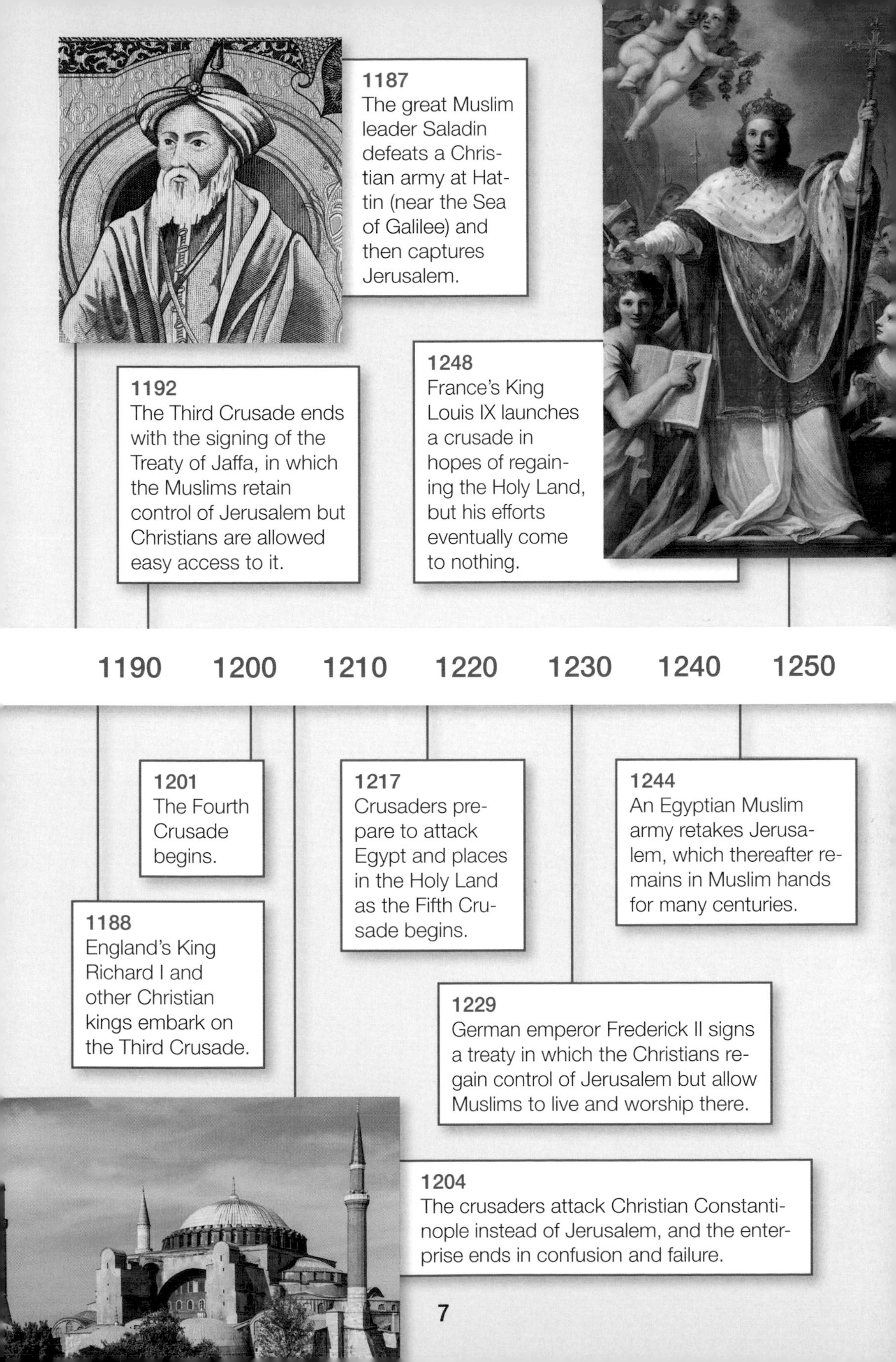
1187
The great Muslim leader Saladin defeats a Christian army at Hattin (near the Sea of Galilee) and then captures Jerusalem.
1192
The Third Crusade ends with the signing of the Treaty of Jaffa, in which the Muslims retain control of Jerusalem but Christians are allowed easy access to it.
1248
France's King Louis IX launches a crusade in hopes of regaining the Holy Land, but his efforts eventually come to nothing.
1190
1200
1210
1220
1230
1240
1250
1201
The Fourth Crusade begins.
1217
Crusaders prepare to attack Egypt and places in the Holy Land as the Fifth Crusade begins.
1244
An Egyptian Muslim army retakes Jerusalem, which thereafter remains in Muslim hands for many centuries.
1188
England's King Richard I and other Christian kings embark on the Third Crusade.
1229
German emperor Frederick II signs a treaty in which the Christians regain control of Jerusalem but allow Muslims to live and worship there.
1204
The crusaders attack Christian Constantinople instead of Jerusalem, and the enterprise ends in confusion and failure.

Chapter One

A Brief History of the Crusades

The Crusades consisted of a succession of military conflicts fought between European Christians and various Muslim groups for control of the Holy Land (now Israel) and surrounding regions. The initial crusading expedition began in 1096, and subsequent ones carried on at intervals for several centuries. Modern historians generally agree that the first five crusades were the most crucial. After that, considerable scholarly disagreement exists over how many such expeditions should be properly labeled *crusades* and even over their exact dates.

One point that all experts agree on is that these attempts to wrest control of the Holy Land from Muslim rule formed a military and cultural milestone. They brought the peoples of the West (Europe) and the Levant (the lands bordering the eastern Mediterranean Sea) into bloody turmoil at the height of the medieval era. The rivalries and bitter feelings created by those wars linger today and continue to color relations between West and East. In the words of a noted scholar of the Crusades, Oxford University's Christopher Tyerman, "The Crusades present a phenomenon so dramatic and extreme in [goals] and execution, and yet so [repulsive] to modern sensibilities, that they cannot fail to move both as a story and as an expression of a society remote in time and attitudes, yet apparently so abundantly recognizable [to modern eyes]."[1]

Motivation and the Call to Arms

The First Crusade launched at the urgings of Pope Urban II at the Council of Clermont in France in November 1095. He was motivated by a series of events that had begun far to the east four decades before. In 1055 the Seljuk Turks, who were Muslims, swept out of Persia (now Iran) into Mesopotamia (now Iraq). Next they raided Anatolia (now Turkey), then part of the Christian Byzantine Empire. The warlike Turks decisively defeated the Byzantines in 1071; that same year Turkish forces seized Jerusalem, in the heart of the Holy Land. After that, the demoralized Byzantines began fighting among themselves, which allowed the invaders to gain considerable ground.

From this Byzantine civil strife eventually arose a new, well-meaning emperor, Alexius I. Hoping to drive the Turks from his lands, in August 1095 he sent a request for military assistance to Urban, who agreed to help. A few months later at Clermont, the pope addressed a large crowd of Christian leaders and vigorously pressed them to aid their beleaguered fellow Christians in Anatolia.

> **"I, or rather the Lord, beseech you . . . to destroy that vile [Turkish] race from the lands of our friends."[2]**
>
> —Pope Urban II, as reported by an eyewitness

At the same time, Urban said, the expedition should free the Holy Land from the Turks. The pope's exact words have not survived. But a few of those who witnessed the speech later pieced together summaries of it. One of them, known as Robert the Monk, recalled the pope's graphic list of vile acts supposedly committed by the Turks. They included torching Christian churches and torturing, beheading, and raping Christians. Urban concluded his oration with a resounding call to arms, as recalled by another witness, Christian priest Fulcher of Chartres: "I, or rather the Lord, beseech you as Christ's heralds to publish this everywhere and to persuade all people of whatever rank, foot-soldiers and knights, poor and rich, to carry aid promptly to those Christians and to destroy that vile race from the lands of our friends. [Moreover], Christ commands it!"[2]

The People's Crusade

Both Urban and Alexius expected that the expedition to the Holy Land would be made up mainly of knights and other trained soldiers. Certainly, many such fighting men began making plans to put their normal lives on hold and head eastward. What the enterprise's leaders did not anticipate was that many ordinary civilians would be inspired to fight and would begin the journey almost immediately.

Indeed, right after Urban's November 1095 call to arms, an up-till-then little-known traveling preacher known as Peter the Hermit answered that call. Moving quickly from town to town, Peter delivered impassioned speeches that gathered him numerous followers in France and elsewhere. By the spring of 1096, they numbered close to one hundred thousand. Later called the People's Crusade, most of its members, historian Thomas F. Madden explains, "were relatively poor, and a great many were armed with only the crudest implements. Many were women and children." Filled with religious fervor, they marched across Europe, driven "by simple faith and Peter's own spellbinding personality." The expedition "could not be slowed, let alone stopped."[3]

When this huge but ragtag band reached the Byzantine capital of Constantinople, Alexius was taken aback. Instead of the trained soldiers he had hoped for, he beheld mostly "common people," according to the twelfth-century Christian historian Albert of Aix. They consisted of "the chaste [uncorrupted] as well as the sinful adulterers, homicides [murderers], thieves, perjurers, and robbers."[4]

Reluctantly, Alexius transported Peter's minions into Anatolia, where Turkish armies were rampant. The battle-hardened Turkish fighters made easy work of these initial crusaders, almost all of whom were slaughtered. Peter himself survived. He was on hand

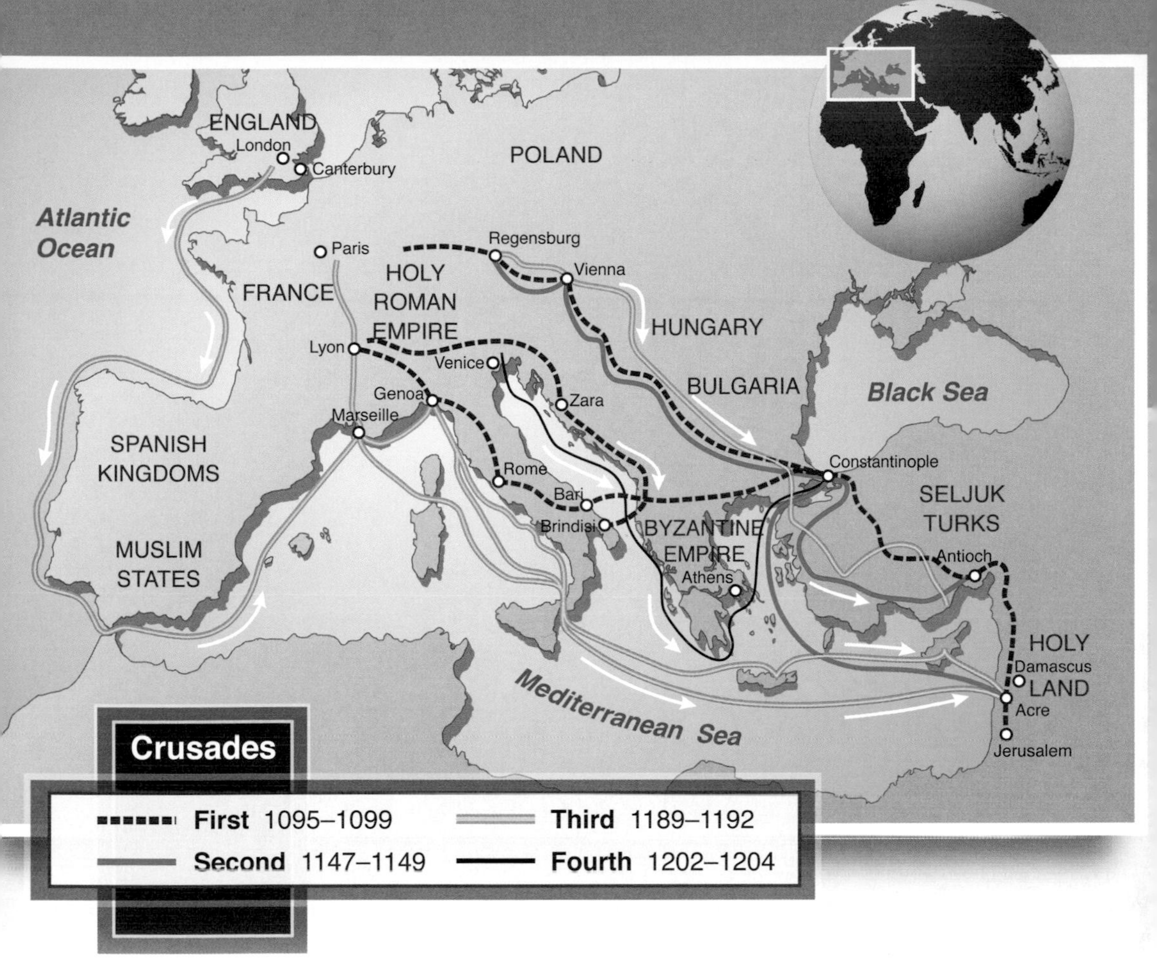

to greet the first groups of trained, armed crusaders when they reached Constantinople in late 1096 and early 1097.

From Anatolia to Jerusalem

Entering the Turkish-held Byzantine lands, the crusaders, at least fifty thousand strong, defeated the Turks at Dorylaeum in northwestern Anatolia and continued eastward. The crusaders found that, although they came from several different nations, the Turks called them all Franks (an early version of "French"), and that name thereafter stuck in the East. One Frankish contingent, led by Baldwin of Boulogne, soon captured Edessa in eastern Anatolia. There, in March 1098, Baldwin established the first of several small European kingdoms in the Levant, collectively called both crusader states and the Outremer (from a French word meaning "overseas").

The bulk of the crusaders continued southward into Syria. They besieged and took the large, well-fortified Syrian city of Antioch and in January 1099 headed for Jerusalem. The siege of that ancient stronghold began in June but did not last long. On July 15 the attackers breached the defenses and entered, as later recalled by Fulcher of Chartres:

> One of the towers in the stone wall began to burn, [and] the flames and smoke soon became so bad that none of the defenders of this part of the wall were able to remain near this place. At the noon hour on Friday, with trumpets sounding, amid great commotion and shouting "God help us," the Franks entered the city. [The] pagans [Muslims] were completely demoralized, and all their former boldness vanished, and they turned to flee through the narrow streets of the city.[5]

For the Christian crusaders, the capture of Jerusalem was the crowning achievement of their venture. They also established three more Outremer kingdoms, centered at Antioch, Tripoli, and Jerusalem. Studded with stone castles, these military outposts were intended to help maintain the Christians' newly acquired grip on the Holy Land.

The Second and Third Crusades

Europeans of that time viewed the ring of security the Outremer provided as so crucial that losing one kingdom was enough to trigger another crusade. In 1144, some four decades after the Christians' seizure of Jerusalem, Zengi, ruler of Turkish-held Mosul (now in Iraq), overran Edessa. In response, Germany's King

Conrad III and France's King Louis VII launched the Second Crusade. They left for the Levant in 1146 with much enthusiasm, but they were unable to make any significant headway there, and the expedition ended in failure two years later.

That lackluster Christian performance emboldened some of the Turkish and other Muslim leaders who held sway in parts of the Middle East. Several dreamed of recapturing Jerusalem, but the first to make a credible attempt was Saladin. In his youth an ordinary soldier, through talent and tenacity he had risen through the ranks to become sultan of Egypt and the Muslim-held portion of Syria. In 1187 Saladin defeated a Christian army at Hattin, near the Sea of Galilee (now in Israel), then seized Jerusalem.

> **"With trumpets sounding, amid great commotion and shouting 'God help us,' the Franks entered the city."[5]**
>
> **—Eleventh-century churchman Fulcher of Chartres**

The reaction to this event in Europe was another round of anger and religious fervor. England's King Richard I (known as the Lionheart), Germany's King Frederick I, and France's King Philip II were the principal leaders of the Third Crusade, which launched in 1188. Their initial zeal swiftly faded, partly because Frederick died on the way to the Levant; later Richard and Philip could not get along, and in 1191 the French ruler abruptly took his army home. Richard managed to defeat Saladin in one large battle that same year but was unable to mount a siege of Jerusalem. The crusade ended with the two opposing leaders signing the Treaty of Jaffa. It largely maintained the status quo while granting Christians easy access to the local sacred sites.

A Dismal Record of Achievement

Of the first three crusades, therefore, only the first one had achieved any sort of clear-cut success, and its positive effects had not lasted long. In general, that dismal record of achievement continued in the Christian crusading expeditions that followed. In the Fourth Crusade (1201–1204), for example, the crusaders never even made it to the Levant. The Fifth Crusade (1217–1229) was also an overall failure.

A bit of Christian headway did occur in the Sixth Crusade (1228–1229). Frederick II, emperor of Germany and Italy, took an army to the Levant, but his soldiers saw almost no action. Instead, he negotiated with the strongest Muslim ruler in the region and acquired Jerusalem and some neighboring towns through a treaty. That gain soon slipped through Christian fingers, however, when an army of Egyptian Muslims recaptured Jerusalem in 1244.

The intermittent, disorganized Christian expeditions that followed came to nothing, while over time the remaining Outremer states fell to Muslim forces. Thereafter, historian Thomas Asbridge points out, no Christian armies "ever reclaimed the Holy City, and Islam's hold over the Levant did not weaken until the early twentieth century."[6] Thus, the Muslims of the late medieval era were sure they had won the series of holy wars that came to be called the Crusades. As one Muslim observer of the time remarked, the Levant "was purified of the Franks" and is "now in Muslim hands." With a mix of triumph and humility, he added, "Praise be to God!"[7]

Chapter Two

Was Retaking the Holy Land the Purpose of the First Crusade?

The First Crusade Was Fought to Retake the Holy Land

- The crusaders were reacting to the occupation of the Holy Land by Muslim armies.
- Christians in the Holy Land were religiously abused, including forced conversion to Islam.
- The Muslim Turks had to be stopped before they used their stronghold in the Holy Land as a springboard to conquer all of Europe.

Retaking the Holy Land Was Not the True Purpose of the First Crusade

- The First Crusade began as an attempt to drive the Turks out of Byzantine-ruled Anatolia, *not* the Holy Land.
- The First Crusade marked the start of Europe's colonial policies—its attempt to exert its control over foreign lands and peoples.
- False narratives and hidden agendas obscured the larger reasons behind the First Crusade.

The First Crusade Was Fought to Retake the Holy Land

"[The Turks] have laid Jerusalem in heaps; the dead bodies of [Christians] have been given to be food for the birds. [We must] advance boldly, as knights of Christ, and rush as quickly as [we] can to the defense of the Eastern Church."

—Pope Urban II

Quoted in August C. Krey, ed., *The First Crusade: The Accounts of Eyewitnesses and Participants*. Charleston, SC: Nabu, 2014, pp. 34–35.

Consider these questions as you read:

1. Why did so many thousands of European Christians answer Pope Urban's call to free the Holy Land from the Turks?
2. How might a person who lived at the time of the Crusades been able to tell truth from fiction or exaggeration from reality, and how might a person living today be able to do the same?
3. How might the world have been different if the Muslim armies that occupied Spain and tried to capture France had conquered all of Europe?

Editor's note: The discussion that follows presents common arguments made in support of this perspective. All arguments are supported by facts, quotes, and examples taken from various sources of the period or present day.

The First Crusade was without doubt fought primarily to retake the Holy Land. In part this was because the crusaders were quite reasonably reacting to the occupation of the Holy Land by Muslim armies. Centered at the sacred city of Jerusalem, the Holy Land was the region where Jesus Christ lived, preached, and died. In addition to the holy sites in Jerusalem itself, several nearby towns, including Bethlehem and Nazareth, contained places and relics sacred and dear to Christianity.

Christians, both in Europe and the East (those living in the Byzantine realm and the Holy Land itself) had long enjoyed visiting these holy places, when time and personal means allowed it. There, in a figurative manner, they walked in the footsteps of Jesus and his disciples. They also more concretely engaged in prayer, gave to the poor, and otherwise paid homage to God. The idea that nonbelievers came to control the sacred sites and to decide whether Christians could visit them was extremely repugnant to those who took part in the First Crusade.

All Sorts of Horrors

Moreover, it was not simply Muslim *control* of the Holy Land that incensed European Christians. In the years immediately following the Turks' capture of Jerusalem and its environs in 1071, disturbing accounts steadily crept into Europe from the East. They described all sorts of horrors perpetrated on Eastern Christians by the Turkish occupiers. In his famous speech delivered at Clermont in 1095, Pope Urban II mentioned some of these outrages. According to one eyewitness account, he said that the "despicable" Turkish race had

> either entirely destroyed the churches of God or appropriated them for the rituals of its own religion. They destroy the altars, after having defiled them with their uncleanness. They circumcise the Christians, and the blood of the circumcision they either spread upon the altars or pour into the vases of the baptismal font. When they wish to torture people by a base death, they perforate their navels, and dragging forth the extremity of the intestines, bind it to a stake; then with flogging they lead the victim around until the viscera [intestines] having gushed forth and the victim falls prostrate upon the ground. Others

> they bind to a post and pierce them with arrows. Others they compel to extend their necks and then, attacking them with naked swords, attempt to cut through the neck with a single blow.[8]

Another account of the awful treatment of Christians by Muslims in the Levant was that of the pope's contemporary, Archbishop Balderic of Dol. With "deep sorrow," he stated, he felt compelled to recount the "dire sufferings" of Eastern Christians. They had been oppressed, whipped, and otherwise punished in Jerusalem, Antioch, and other Christian places. Indeed, Balderic said, many Christian residents of that region had been driven from their homes. Those dispossessed folk

> **"Attacking [Eastern Christians] with naked swords, [the Turks] attempt to cut through the neck with a single blow."[8]**
>
> **—Pope Urban II, as reported by an eyewitness**

> come as beggars among us; or, which is far worse, they are flogged and exiled as slaves for sale in their own land. Christian blood, redeemed by the blood of Christ, has been shed, and Christian flesh, akin to the flesh of Christ, has been subjected to unspeakable degradation and servitude. Everywhere in those cities there is sorrow, everywhere misery, everywhere groaning. [The] churches in which divine mysteries were celebrated in olden times are now, to our sorrow, used as stables for the animals of these people [the Turks]![9]

Religious Abuses

Among the worst acts reported from the occupied Holy Land were religious abuses the Turks meted out to Christians and Jews. In theory, the Muslim Turks should have respected the Christians'

European monarchs embarked on the First Crusade to free the Holy Land from Muslim control. The retaking of Jerusalem in 1099, depicted here, marked Europe's success and led to the founding of Christian colonies—crusader states—in the region.

and Jews' faiths. After all, the three religions recognize Abraham as their founding prophet, plus Muslims view Moses and Jesus as prophets as well.

Yet according to Urban and other Christian leaders of that time, Turks regularly penalized Christians and Jews for their beliefs. Under Turkish rule, it was said, Christians could not ride horses, which were reserved for Muslims. Christians could ride only mules, apparently to symbolize their second-class and supposedly misguided religious beliefs. Similarly, Christians had to wear certain insignia on their outer clothing to mark them apart from Muslims. In some cities Christians could not carry weapons, whereas Muslims could. And Christians had to pay extra taxes as a penalty for their beliefs.

Worst of all, the pope and other Christian officials claimed that over time the Turks forced large numbers of Eastern Christians to convert to Islam. In some cases, the story went, Christians were offered a choice: either accept Islam or face execution. To legally support this and the other religious abuses, local Turkish authorities fell back on very conservative interpretations of passages from Islam's sacred book, the Quran. One states, "The Christians call Christ the son of God. That is but a saying from their mouth; in this, they but imitate what the unbelievers of old used to say. God's curse be on them; how they are deluded away from the Truth! . . . They take as their Lord Christ the son of Mary. Yet they were commanded to worship but One God. There is no god but He."[10]

The Turkish religious authorities took this to mean that the Christians' worship of Jesus and belief that he was God's son showed disrespect for God. Only God should be worshipped; moreover, God had no son, the authorities insisted. The Turks saw treating God in this manner as an act so wicked that any Christians who did it must be punished. The lucky ones, reports from the East suggested, could not ride horses or carry weapons, while others faced the choice of converting or dying, and at least some chose execution over conversion. European Christians were appalled by these religious abuses, and for many that alone was reason to join the pope's expedition to retake the Holy Land from the Muslims.

A Smart Preventative Move

From a military standpoint, this campaign also represented an important strategic move. A great deal of evidence existed to indicate that seizing the Holy Land would not be the Turks' and other Muslims' final round of conquest. In fact, in the late eleventh century, there was every reason to believe their ultimate goal was to overrun Europe and eventually the entire known world. Put simply, some Christian leaders of that time felt that the wave of Muslim expansion had to be stopped before it rolled across France, Germany, and other Christian nations.

The belief that this danger was real rested on the argument that future Islamic expansion would be a continuation of a policy formulated centuries before. Shortly after Islam's founder, the Prophet Muhammad, passed away in 632, his followers swept out of Arabia. Little by little they captured large tracts of Middle Eastern territory. These early Muslim conquerors were filled with zeal, based on "an unwavering feeling of supremacy and buoyant conviction" in Islam's "ultimate triumph," historian Efraim Karsh explains. The Arab militarists "acted in a typically imperialist fashion from the start."[11]

Indeed, after overrunning most of the Middle East in the mid-600s, Muslim armies headed outward in different directions. Some moved eastward into central Asia. Others made their way westward across coastal North Africa, and not long after 700 that entire region was under Muslim control. But Islamic expansion did not end there. In 711 Muslim soldiers crossed the Strait of Gibraltar into southern Spain. There they routed a force of local Christians who had gathered in hopes of halting the invasion. In a mere two years, the invaders controlled nearly all of Spain.

"[Muslim conquerors] acted in a typically imperialist fashion from the start."[11]

—Historian Efraim Karsh

The rest of Europe must now have attracted Muslim leaders. In 718 they sent large raiding parties into Francia—the area inhabited by the original Frankish people—which would later become France. The invaders seized town after town and by 725 had reached a point only 200 miles (322 km) south of Paris. Worried that the Muslims might conquer all of Francia, the natives struck back in force. Commanded by a military leader named Charles Martel, in 732 the Franks decisively defeated the intruders, who retreated back into Spain.

Some three centuries later, the French and other Europeans remembered the threat that Muslim armies had once posed. In 1095, therefore, driving the Muslims out of the Holy Land seemed like a smart move. While liberating Jerusalem and its sacred sites, it would ultimately keep Europe safe.

Retaking the Holy Land Was Not the True Purpose of the First Crusade

"On a spiritual and moral level, the Crusades offered the chance to redirect militant passions of the knightly class of Europe into what was seen as being a truly noble quest, thereby helping countless men to save their souls and improve their moral dispositions."

—Suffolk University scholar Christopher Libertini

Christopher Libertini, "Crusaders Were Motivated by Political Considerations as Well as the Promise of Spiritual Rewards and Increased Social Prestige," in *World History in Context* (database), Gale, 2003. http://ic.galegroup.com/ic/whic/ReferenceDetailsPage/ReferenceDetailsWindow?zid=5ce04720240d6edc41ece33a60c2fc96&action=2&catId=&documentId=GALE%7CCX2877000020&userGroupName=tlc199095657&jsid=4a457e60f27cda06521b9794259c49f7.

Consider these questions as you read:

1. How might the public have responded to the call for a crusade if it had been explained as a colonial venture or a play for greater power by the pope?
2. Do you agree with the idea that the First Crusade was Europe's first colonial venture? Why or why not?
3. How might the course of events have differed if stories of cooperation between Muslims and Christians in the Holy Land had replaced stories of atrocities?

Editor's note: The discussion that follows presents common arguments made in support of this perspective. All arguments are supported by facts, quotes, and examples taken from various sources of the period or present day.

Retaking the Holy Land was not the actual purpose of the First Crusade. First, the idea of European armies liberating the Holy Land from Turkish control was not what Urban, the conflict's instigator, originally had in mind. In recruiting Christian soldiers for an expedition to the East, he actually had two other initial goals.

Urban and the Christian Cosmos

One of those aims was to help Alexius I, emperor of the Byzantine Empire, centered at Constantinople (situated just south of the Black Sea). In March 1095 Urban oversaw a meeting of churchmen in northern Italy. In the midst of the gathering, a Byzantine messenger arrived with a message for the Christian pontiff. Opening it, Urban found an urgent plea for aid from Alexius.

The Byzantine emperor and his subjects did not answer to the pope and Western Christian church; rather, the Byzantines followed the Eastern Orthodox version of Christianity. Yet whether Western or Eastern, all were devoted followers of Jesus Christ, and each side felt an obligation to help the other in times of dire need.

This, Alexius told Urban, was just such a time. Ever since the Turks had defeated the Byzantines in a major battle in 1071, the emperor explained, his realm had been afflicted. The Turks had steadily expanded their power base in Anatolia, which had originally been Byzantine territory. Alexius feared that the enemy would soon attack Constantinople itself and then move into Europe. If the pope could rally some troops to help the Byzantines, the emperor said, it would ultimately benefit Italy and other European nations by keeping the Turks from invading Europe.

On this point, Urban saw the wisdom of mounting an expedition to aid Alexius. The pope also realized how such a venture might benefit his own position as Europe's spiritual leader. In his mind, historian Thomas Asbridge asserts, Urban began to see how an "armed pilgrimage to the East" could "fulfill a broader array of ambitions." It presented "a chance not only to defend [Byzantine Christians] and improve relations with the Greek Church, but also to reaffirm and expand Rome's authority. [The] grand scheme would be launched as part of a broader campaign to extend the reach of papal influence beyond the confines of central Italy, into Urban's birthplace and homeland, France."[12]

The eminently practical Urban was well aware that he could not mention his personal, selfish ambitions when raising Western

This image shows Pope Urban II announcing the First Crusade in 1095. Urban viewed the campaign both as a means to foil Muslim ambitions to invade Europe and as an opportunity to grow the power of the Roman Church and his own position as its head.

Christian armies. He also wagered that aiding the Byzantines alone might not arouse the passion to fight among many European lords and knights. The "grand scheme" had to have a more alluring motivation. So, "in a visionary masterstroke," in Asbridge's words, the pope suggested that the Turks must be stopped not only to help Alexius but also for a more compelling reason. Urban "broadened his appeal to include an additional target, one guaranteed to stir Frankish hearts," explains Asbridge. "Fusing the ideals of warfare and pilgrimage, he unveiled an expedition that would forge a path to the Holy Land itself, there to win back possession of Jerusalem, the most hallowed site in the Christian cosmos."[13] Therefore, the First Crusade was not initially intended to free the Holy Land from

Turkish oppression. Instead, the war was designed to strengthen the Byzantine emperor's position, along with Urban's own power base within European Christendom.

Colonies and Booty

Although the lure of regaining control of the Holy Land was a powerful magnet for crusaders, the First Crusade actually had a broader purpose: colonization. Historians often say that the modern colonial period began after Europeans discovered the Americas. Spain, France, England, and other European nations colonized large parts of the globe and for a long time exploited foreign peoples. European colonialism did not start in the 1500s and 1600s, however, states popular British writer Karen Armstrong. It actually began between 1096 and 1099, the years of the First Crusade. In 1983 Armstrong visited Israel and toured the sites of some of the Christian strongholds erected during the era of the First Crusade—the so-called crusader states. "They were our first colonies," she later wrote, speaking as a European. "I was particularly struck by the crusaders' massive castles and fortresses, [which] were built all along the borders of their states. There was a chain of crusader castles in Israel, Lebanon, Syria, and Jordan." She explained that the castles were absolutely necessary to defend and maintain those early European colonies that had suddenly arisen "in a hostile Muslim world."[14]

> **"Fusing the ideals of warfare and pilgrimage, [Pope Urban] unveiled an expedition that would forge a path to the Holy Land."[13]**
>
> **—Historian Thomas Asbridge**

In a very real way, that made the First Crusade Europe's first colonial war. Historian Thomas F. Madden explains that in this view, the conflict was "a kind of proto-imperialism visited on the Muslim people. Men with little to lose and everything to gain" seemingly "took the [Christian] cross merely as a pious pretext to enrich themselves with stolen booty and carve out a new home in a distant land."[15]

Certainly, the lure of establishing colonies in the Holy Land and using them as bases from which to raid and plunder the riches of the East was strong among many European landed nobles. Several early modern historians noted this factor, among them German scholar Johann von Mosheim. In the mid-1700s, he wrote that the European crusaders "learned by experience that these holy wars contributed much to increase their opulence [wealth] and to extend their authority."[16]

Mosheim's opinion that greed was a major motivation for the crusaders was echoed later by his younger contemporary, the great English historian Edward Gibbon. Large numbers of crusaders were after loot, Gibbon wrote. They hoped to find "mines of treasures, of gold and diamonds" in the Levant. They had heard rumors of splendid "palaces of marble and jasper, and of [fragrant] groves of [rare spices, including] cinnamon and frankincense."[17]

But one need not take only the word of modern historians who researched the First Crusade between the 1700s and today. The incentive to go on a major expedition to the Levant for the sake of colonies and booty came from Urban's own lips. According to one medieval source, he told those assembled at Clermont, "Enter upon the road to the Holy Sepulchre [Jesus's tomb in Jerusalem]; wrest that land from the wicked race, and subject it to yourselves. That land which as the Scripture says 'flows with milk and honey,' was given by God into the possession of the children of Israel. [The] land [around Jerusalem] is fruitful above others, like another paradise of delights."[18]

In another account from that era, Urban reportedly promised various material rewards to those soldiers who would go on the crusade. "The possessions of the enemy, too, will be yours," the pope said. "You will make spoil of their treasures and return victorious to your own [possessions]."[19]

Blatant Lies

Even the primary justification given for retaking the Holy Land—that Jerusalem's Christian inhabitants were being mistreated by their Muslim occupiers—was false. In fact, with a few exceptions, Turkish authorities were reasonably tolerant toward the Christians under their rule. The accusations of severe intolerance and brutality were blatant lies used by the pope to convince European knights and others to join the crusading expedition. For reasons that remain unclear, the Muslim authorities in the region of Jerusalem did close down a few Christian churches in the eleventh century. But most Christian houses of worship remained intact.

Moreover, as long as they did not disparage Muslims and Islam, Christians themselves were left unmolested. In large part this was because the authorities tried to follow the dictates of the Muslim holy book, the Quran. It states plainly, "You disbelievers, I worship not what you worship, nor do you worship whom I worship. Neither shall I worship what you worship, nor will you worship whom I worship. To you be your religion, and to me my religion."[20]

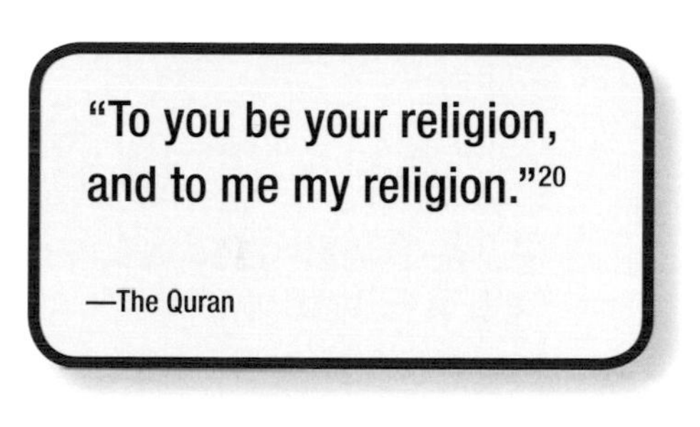

Noted modern historian Steven Runciman confirms that fact. "In the middle of the eleventh century," he writes, "the lot of Christians in [the Holy Land] had seldom been so pleasant. The Muslim authorities were lenient." Moreover, "never before had Jerusalem enjoyed so plentifully the sympathy and the wealth that were brought to it by the [Christian] pilgrims from the West."[21] Thus, false narratives and hidden agendas obscured the larger reasons behind the First Crusade.

Chapter Three

Did the Crusaders Commit Atrocities?

The Crusaders Committed Atrocities

- On their way to the Holy Land, crusaders brutally slaughtered thousands of European Jews.
- Crusaders butchered many thousands of men, women, and children after capturing Jerusalem in 1099.
- After capturing the village of Maarat al-Numen, crusaders killed and ate several of the residents.

The Crusaders Committed No Acts That Can Be Labeled Atrocities

- Those killed after Jerusalem's fall brought death on themselves by refusing to surrender when that option was offered.
- The people who committed the mass murders of Jews were misguided rabble, not official crusaders.
- The crusaders often demonstrated heroics rather than committed atrocities.

The Crusaders Committed Atrocities

"[The crusaders] did not spare anyone, not even those pleading for mercy. The crowd was struck to the ground, just as rotten fruit falls from shaken branches."

—Eleventh-century churchman Fulcher of Chartres

Quoted in Edward Peters, ed., *The First Crusade: The Chronicle of Fulcher of Chartres and Other Source Materials*. Philadelphia: University of Pennsylvania Press, 1998, pp. 91–92.

Consider these questions as you read:

1. How would you define *atrocity*, and would that definition change in the context of war? Explain your answers.
2. Why do you think groups of crusaders attacked unarmed civilian populations, and could these actions have been prevented? Explain your answer.
3. If you were the commander of the soldiers attacking Jerusalem in 1099, what orders would you have given your soldiers regarding what to do once the walls were breached? Explain why.

Editor's note: The discussion that follows presents common arguments made in support of this perspective. All arguments are supported by facts, quotes, and examples taken from various sources of the period or present day.

European crusaders who invaded the Levant in the eleventh and twelfth centuries committed horrible atrocities in the name of God. Among the worst of those crimes were the massacres of large numbers of Jews by Christians on their way to the Holy Land. The most notorious incidents of this nature occurred during the First Crusade, in its initial phase—the so-called People's Crusade.

That venture actually consisted of multiple expeditions, each following closely on the heels of the preceding one. First, in France in late 1095 and early 1096, the influential preacher Peter the Hermit brought together tens of thousands of zealous Christian believers, a majority of them poor. The knights and other professional warriors that Pope Urban II hoped to send to the Holy Land were still gathering. Peter felt that they were taking too long. At least some Christians, he decided, should strike at the Turks in the Levant as soon as possible.

The Rabid Jew Haters

In April 1096 Peter led the first group of his followers eastward from France into Germany. While in Germany he gave a number of public speeches that brought thousands of German Christians into his fold, after which he swiftly moved on, bound for the Holy Land. In his wake came a splinter group of the People's Crusade. It was led by Count Emicho of Flonheim, a minor German noble who was a vicious anti-Semite. To Emicho, all non-Christians—whether Muslims, Jews, or anyone else—were scum who must be wiped from the face of the earth. Unwittingly, Peter had given Emicho a platform and the power to put his genocidal desires into practice.

In early May 1096 Emicho and his followers entered Speyer in western Germany. There they singled out twelve Jews and ordered them to convert to Christianity immediately. When the twelve refused, Emicho's henchmen killed them where they stood. Moving on to the German town of Worms, the crusaders did not even offer local Jews the choice to convert. The intruders simply slaughtered hundreds of Jews—men, women, and children.

This killing spree continued, reaching its awful peak in another German city, Mainz, which was renowned as a center of Jewish learning and business. When Emicho arrived there in late May, he found the town gates locked securely. At first it appeared that the crusaders would not be able to get in. On May 26, however, a zealous Christian resident opened the gates, allowing the rabid Jew haters to gain entrance.

In a horrendous display of greed and inhumanity, the crusaders made their way through the streets, looting Jewish homes and killing any Jews they found. Even some Christian homes were ransacked and plundered of their valuables. A large group of frightened Jews took refuge in the main hall of the palace of the local bishop, but that turned out to provide no protection. According to the twelfth-century Christian historian Albert of Aix, the marauding Christians "attacked the Jews in the hall with arrows and lances. Breaking the bolts and doors, they killed the Jews, about seven hundred in number, who in vain resisted the force and attack of so many thousands. They killed the women, also, and with their swords pierced tender children of whatever age and sex."[22]

While Europe's monarchs were slow to act, Peter the Hermit, a French priest, urged commoners to lead a People's Crusade eastward in April 1096. However, some mobs used the pro-Christian rhetoric of Peter's rallies to justify killing hundreds of Jews in German cities along the way.

During the slaughter, when it was clear to the last couple of hundred Jews that they were all doomed, they resorted to a desperate, tragic move. In Albert's words, they "fell upon one another, brother, children, wives, and sisters, and thus they perished at each other's hands. Horrible to say, mothers cut the throats of nursing children with knives and stabbed others, preferring them to perish thus by their own hands rather than to be killed by the weapons of the [murderous Christians]."[23]

> **"[The crusaders] had slaughtered the exiled Jews through greed of money, rather than for the sake of God's justice."[24]**
>
> **—Medieval Christian historian Albert of Aix**

Clearly disturbed by these atrocities, Albert was moved to remark that Emicho and his followers "had slaughtered the exiled Jews through greed of money, rather than for the sake of God's justice." God, the historian asserted, "is a just judge and orders no one unwillingly, or under compulsion, to come under the yoke of the Catholic faith."[24]

The Jerusalem Massacre

Other crusaders committed other atrocities during their attacks on the Turkish-ruled Levant. One of the most infamous of these dark deeds was the massacre of most of the population of Jerusalem immediately after the Christians captured the city in July 1099. No sooner had the crusaders breached the walls when, according to the eyewitness account of crusader Guibert of Nogent, the Christian "army ran amok."[25]

The unprovoked slaughter of thousands of men, women, children, and even infants went on for most of the night. After a while, wrote another witness, Raymond of Aguilers, "Piles of heads, hands, and feet were to be seen in the streets of the city. It was necessary to pick one's way over the bodies of men and horses. But these were small matters compared to what happened at the Temple of Solomon, a place where religious services are ordinarily chanted. [There, Christian soldiers] rode in blood up to their knees and bridle reins."[26] In the morning, sunlight made the extent of the butchery clear. One could see, Guibert wrote, that Jerusalem's streets were "filled with so many corpses that the Franks were unable to move without stepping on dead bodies."[27]

As if the mass murders of the preceding hours were not enough, the crusaders continued their rampage. First, there was a despicable display of pillage and disrespect for the dead by several of the lower-class members of the victorious army. According to Fulcher of Chartres, "It was an extraordinary thing to see our squires and poorer people split the bellies of those dead Turks, so that they might pick out besants [gold coins] from their intestines, which they had swallowed down their horrible gullets while alive."[28]

"Our squires and poorer people split the bellies of those dead Turks, so that they might pick out besants [gold coins] from their intestines."[28]

—Christian churchman Fulcher of Chartres

Meanwhile, because the dead bodies choked the narrow streets so tightly, the few surviving Turks were ordered to carry the corpses outside the city. It took a few days to complete this task. Then, following the orders of their commanders, Christian soldiers fell upon and cut to pieces the hapless Turks who had labored so hard to clear the streets. One high-placed crusader, Raymond of Toulouse, condemned the slaughter but was unable to stop it.

The Grisly Events at Marrat

In sheer numbers of innocent civilians slain by crusaders, the mass killing of thousands at Jerusalem in 1099 holds the record. Yet for the grisly, stomach-turning variety of atrocity, it is hard to surpass what happened in Syria the year before. As one group of crusaders marched southward toward Jerusalem, in late November

1098 it came to the Syrian city of Marrat al-Numen. The Christians did not even offer to spare the residents' lives if they surrendered. Instead, the crusaders immediately laid siege to the town.

During that operation, there occurred an incident that can only be described as twisted and revolting. In his account of the First Crusade, Fulcher of Chartres stated, "When the siege [of Marrat] had lasted twenty days, our people suffered excessive hunger. I shudder to tell that many of our people, harassed by the madness of excessive hunger, cut pieces from the buttocks of the Muslims already dead there, which they cooked, but when it was not yet roasted enough by the fire, they devoured it with savage mouth."[29]

This event is one of the few well-documented historical cases of cannibalism in warfare. It should be noted that not all of the Christians then in the Holy Land approved of it. In fact, another surviving account from that era says that "this spectacle disgusted as many crusaders as it did"[30] the Levant's inhabitants—Muslims, Jews, and Christians alike.

To make matters worse, the crusaders besieging Marrat followed up this atrocity with another. After a few weeks, they wore down the town's residents and then attacked in full force. "In an assault of great boldness," Fulcher of Chartres recalled, the "Franks entered over the top of the wall. On that day and the following, they killed all the Muslims, from the greatest [richest] to the least [poorest], and plundered all their substance [belongings]."[31] These heinous incidents at Marrat, like those in Germany and Jerusalem, prove beyond any doubt that the crusaders routinely committed terrible atrocities in the name of God.

The Crusaders Committed No Acts That Can Be Labeled Atrocities

"The slaughter that took place [at] Jerusalem in 1099 has become notorious, partly because later Muslim sources exaggerated the event in order to whip up the spirit of jihad."

—Historian John France

John France, "Impelled by the Love of God," in *Crusades: The Illustrated History*, ed. Thomas F. Madden. Ann Arbor: University of Michigan Press, 2007, p. 47.

Consider these questions as you read:

1. Should historical events be judged according to the standards and values of the time period in which they occurred or by current standards and values? Explain your answer.
2. How strong is the argument that the inhabitants of Jerusalem are to blame for their own deaths because they refused to surrender when given the chance? Explain your answer.
3. Medieval Muslim scholar Usama ibn Munqidh's account criticizes the crusaders but also praises some of them when warranted. Why is it important for historical observers to be as unbiased as possible?

Editor's note: The discussion that follows presents common arguments made in support of this perspective. All arguments are supported by facts, quotes, and examples taken from various sources of the period or present day.

The European Christians who took part in the Crusades were sometimes heavy handed and even brutal. Those expeditions *were* wars, after all, and all wars are bloody and destructive. Nevertheless, the crusaders committed no acts that can be defined as atrocities by the standards of that era. Keep in mind that even if certain violent acts are viewed as atrocities and war crimes today, it does not follow that they were seen that way then.

The Rule of War

The fall of Jerusalem to the crusaders in July 1099 is an example of an event that can be seen in different ways. Some people view the slaughter of some of the city's residents during its capture as an out-and-out atrocity. Yet in truth, those whom the Christian soldiers attacked and killed brought that calamity on themselves. Like people all across Europe and the Middle East in that period, they were well aware of what was often called "the rule of war" or "normal business of war" in relation to siege warfare. As Baylor University scholar Rodney Stark explains:

> If a city did not surrender when given the chance, forcing the attackers to take the city by storm, [the] inhabitants could expect to be massacred as an example to others in the future. That is, had the Muslims surrendered Jerusalem on June 13, when the [siege] towers were ready to be rolled against the walls, they no doubt would have been given terms that would have prevented a massacre.[32]

Thus, by refusing to give up when they had the opportunity, Jerusalem's residents in a very real sense signed their own death warrants. Moreover, a similar rule of medieval warfare has frequently been stated "to the victor go the spoils." That is, looting a captured city was to be expected. Indeed, even if the inhabitants did surrender, they still had to pay a "settlement," constituting a certain proportion of their wealth. They could either pay it that way and live or refuse to surrender and pay it in the form of looting after the attackers killed them.

Another reason that the violence at Jerusalem was not the huge atrocity often alleged is that the number of residents the crusaders slew was not nearly as high as often cited. Muslim historians of that era estimated that some seventy thousand innocent civilians were slaughtered after the crusaders entered the city. That figure continued to enter history books—both in the East and West—for centuries to come.

Only in the twentieth century did Western scholars agree that Muslim writers exaggerated the killings in an attempt to promote jihad, or holy war, against Europeans. Historian John France says that "the slaughter was not total."[33] Rather, he adds, many Muslims escaped. For a while, Western experts accepted a figure of ten thousand killed at the close of the siege.

Yet even that number is too high, it turns out. Historian Thomas Asbridge reports that "recent research has uncovered close contemporary Hebrew testimony that indicates that casualties may not have exceeded 3,000, and that large numbers of prisoners were taken when Jerusalem fell. This suggests that even in the Middle Ages, the image of the crusaders' brutality in 1099 was subject to hyperbole [exaggeration] and manipulation on both sides of the divide."[34] Thus, the atrocities that are often ascribed to Jerusalem's fall during the Crusades were not nearly as horrific as what is often portrayed. It was "certainly accompanied by terrible bloodshed," France admits, "but not by all the imagined horrors of later generations."[35]

"Even in the Middle Ages, the image of the crusaders' brutality in 1099 was subject to hyperbole [exaggeration]."[34]

—Historian Thomas Asbridge

Misguided Rabble

Later manipulation of facts and figures also surrounds a different set of atrocities frequently attributed to some of the crusaders. The events in question consist of the mass murders of European Jews in 1096, mainly in Germany. First, it must be emphasized that the perpetrators of those crimes were not official crusaders—that is, they were not professional knights and other soldiers raised by Urban. Instead, the individuals who slaughtered so many Jews were part of a contingent of misguided rabble carrying out the orders of an appalling anti-Semitic, Emicho of Flonheim. The pope certainly

This manuscript illustrates Christian soldiers pillaging the holy city in 1099. In medieval times, commoners and kings understood that cities taken by conquest were usually looted and their citizens often massacred by rule of war.

did not approve of such actions. In fact, he publicly and "harshly condemned the killings," as scholar Thomas F. Madden points out. After the fact, however, "there was little more that he could do."[36]

Furthermore, other high-placed Christian churchmen actually risked life and limb in efforts to stop the murders instigated by Emicho. "It is important to note that almost everywhere," the late, respected Jewish French historian Leon Poliakov wrote, "bishops attempted, sometimes at the peril of their own lives, to protect the Jews."[37]

At Speyer, for instance, the reason that only twelve Jews were murdered is that the local bishop intervened. He placed dozens of others under his protection, as well as ordered some of his Christian followers to track down and capture as many of Emicho's henchmen as possible. This was done, and the bishop ordered the prisoners' hands to be cut off as a punishment. Similar interventions by bishops occurred at Cologne, Metz, and other German towns that Emicho terrorized. These incidents show clearly that murdering Jews was not the policy of the Catholic Church and its crusaders.

Even a number of Christian knights independently fought murderous mobs of anti-Semites and saved numerous Jews in the process. One mob led by a homicidal priest named Volkmar crossed from Germany into Hungary and started pillaging Jewish homes. Suddenly, a force of Hungarian Christian knights appeared and killed the intruders on the spot. Soon afterward some of Emicho's followers tried to hunt down Hungarian Jews, and the same knights slew several of the anti-Semites and beat the rest back over the border. The destruction of most of Emicho's and Volkmar's Jew-hating adherents by Christians impressed Christians across Europe. "To most good Christians," historian Steven Runciman writes, "it appeared as a punishment meted out from on high [from God] to the murderers of the Jews."[38]

Giving the Franks Their Due

Not only did the crusaders routinely refrain from committing out-and-out atrocities, they quite often demonstrated the opposite kind of behavior. That is, they frequently displayed uncommon courage and even heroic acts in the midst of combat. Even some Muslim observers were impressed and later penned accounts designed to give those brave crusaders their due.

Among those observers, one of the more reliable and colorful was Usama ibn Munqidh. Of Syrian birth, he was well educated and became a respected soldier, diplomat, and scholar. For a while he worked for the famous Muslim military leader Saladin and witnessed various episodes of the Third Crusade (1188–1192) firsthand. Like other Muslims of that time, Ibn Munqidh considered the crusaders, whom he called Franks, crude interlopers. Yet he described their strengths when the situation called for it.

For example, after a Frankish contingent defeated Ibn Munqidh and his companions in a skirmish, he wrote, "The Franks (God curse them) are the most cautious of all men in war."[39] This compliment was followed by a completely candid description of how the Franks had gotten the better of Ibn Munqidh's group.

On several occasions Ibn Munqidh singled out acts of bravery performed by Frankish knights. In one encounter, a contingent of Franks was camped on one side of a river, and a group of Muslim fighters was camped on the other. In a surprise move, the Muslims crossed the river and surrounded the Frankish camp. A few minutes later, Ibn Munqidh wrote, "suddenly a lone Frankish horseman came forth and charged our men until he got right into their midst, so they killed his charger [horse] and wounded him mercilessly. But he continued to fight on foot until he made it back to his comrades."[40] Perhaps out of respect for this valiant show, the Muslim commander ordered his soldiers to withdraw, despite their military advantage.

"Suddenly a lone Frankish horseman came forth and charged our men until he got right into their midst."[40]

—Twelfth-century Muslim scholar Usama ibn Munqidh

Later, during a momentary truce, Ibn Munqidh met that knight face-to-face and was impressed with his noble bearing and decency. "He was a good-looking, well-dressed youth," Ibn Munqidh recalled. "He bore the marks of multiple wounds," including on his face "the mark of sword-blow that cut him from the top of his head to the middle of his face."[41] Ibn Munqidh then remarked how God works in mysterious ways. Although the Franks were unwanted invaders, he seemed to imply, God let the young Frank live because of his courage. In his long, detailed book, Ibn Munqidh described many other incidents involving the Franks, and not once did he mention them committing an atrocity. If there had been any, surely he would have mentioned them.

Chapter Four

Were the Crusades More Brutal than Other Medieval Wars?

The Crusades Were More Brutal than Other Medieval Wars

- Religious zeal and desire for land drove the crusaders to the commission of often brutal, barbaric acts.
- The Crusades were particularly brutal because the Christian soldiers sought to eradicate Arabs, Turks, and other Muslims.
- The crusaders felt they had to be more violent than normal because they were badly outnumbered by the enemy.

The Crusades Were Not More Brutal than Other Medieval Wars

- Europeans waged war in the Holy Land no differently than they did at home.
- The Crusades were too poorly planned and disorganized to produce a higher-than-normal level of brutality.
- Most crusaders felt they had no need to be more brutal than normal, because they had plenty of soldiers and supplies.

The Crusades Were More Brutal than Other Medieval Wars

"The crusaders were insensible to pity. For several days they enacted the worst scenes of outrage and spoliation [looting], within and without the walls of Constantinople."

—Scholars G.W. Foote and J.M. Wheeler

G.W. Foote and J.M. Wheeler, *Crimes of Christianity*. London: Progressive, 1887, p. 173.

Consider these questions as you read:

1. How did religion influence the ferocity of crusader warfare?
2. What other factors influenced the vicious nature of the Crusades?
3. How strong is the argument that the Crusades were aimed at committing genocide? Explain your answer.

Editor's note: The discussion that follows presents common arguments made in support of this perspective. All arguments are supported by facts, quotes, and examples taken from various sources of the period or present day.

The Crusades were, on the whole, definitely more vicious and cruel than most other medieval conflicts. One of the leading reasons for this was the sad fact that large numbers of crusaders were infected with unrestrained and undisciplined religious zeal. In addition, a great many were filled with uncontrollable greed for new land to exploit. (In the medieval era, land ownership was synonymous with wealth and high social status.) These traits—religious fervor and greed—taken to extremes, often drove the crusaders to commit brutal, barbaric acts against their Muslim enemies.

Promises of Paradise

In the words of the late scholar G.W. Foote, "Religious fanaticism was the chief motive"[42] of the First Crusade. This religious extremism, which brought about so much excessive hostility and violence, came in large part from the crusaders' belief that God needed and wanted them to fight for him. Because he supposedly sanctified the expeditions to the Holy Land, whatever they did there would be in his name.

Moreover, God could be counted on to forgive *any* acts the crusaders might commit there that would normally be seen as horrible deeds. Foote points out that in Pope Urban II's famous speech at Clermont in 1095, he "promised a remission of sins to those who joined" the expedition and "paradise to those who fell in battle. Christ's saying 'I come not to bring peace but a sword' was to be verified [during the crusade], and the cross was to be the symbol of bloodshed." To remind themselves that brutal killing was their main aim, many of the crusaders wore red crosses. "The most frenzied crusaders cut the holy sign on the flesh itself,"[43] according to Foote.

"The most frenzied crusaders cut the holy sign on the flesh itself."[43]

—Scholar G.W. Foote

Hardened soldiers who were so programmed by religious propaganda that they permanently disfigured themselves were driven to commit acts more brutal than in previous conflicts. Urban's plea for Christians to kill and maim non-Christians found many willing participants. As the great British historian Edward Gibbon said, "At the voice of their pastor, the robber, the [arsonist, and] the murderer, arose by thousands to redeem their souls." They were convinced they could do this by "repeating on the infidels," or Muslims, the same violent deeds the crusaders had perpetrated on "their Christian brethren"[44] in the past, only more so.

Stricken by Land Hunger

Magnifying this spiritually driven bloodlust was an intense hunger to acquire new and valuable land. This greed was also sanctioned by the pope and other churchmen. "The papacy was taking over the direction" of these holy wars, noted historian Steven Runciman explains. "The land that was conquered had to be held under ultimate papal suzerainty [control]."[45] In other words, the church would have a say in how any lands the crusaders captured in the Levant would be governed and utilized. So it was in the interest of church leaders to encourage the conquest of such lands.

This suited the Christian soldiers, especially the sons of well-to-do lords who already owned land, perfectly well. These second-generation nobles became stricken by an insidious "land-

During a council meeting in Clermont in 1095, the pope assured the assembled church leaders that God would forgive the sins of those undertaking the crusade.

hunger," Runciman says. It was rooted in the existing land and inheritance laws in France and elsewhere in Europe, which were also based in extreme greed. "As a lord became unwilling to divide his property, [his] younger sons had to seek their fortunes elsewhere," Runciman explains. "There was a general restlessness and taste for adventure in the knightly class in France, [and] the opportunity for combining Christian duty with the acquisition of land in a southern climate was very attractive."[46]

So desperate were these young men for their own land that they were willing to commit any acts, no matter how brutal. In the Third Crusade, for example, those acts included the slaughter of unarmed civilians, defiling the bodies in various ways, and engaging with prostitutes on a scale never seen in European wars. "The vices and disorders of the crusaders were so disgraceful," Foote wrote, "that the authors of the old [medieval] chronicles blushed while they retraced the pictures of them."[47]

Primitive Barbarism

Another reason the Crusades were particularly brutal by the standards of medieval European warfare was that the barbaric Christian soldiers sought not simply to defeat and chase away Turks and other Muslims. In many cases the crusaders' goal was to eradicate them—to commit what people today call genocide. Indeed, says Saudi scholar Abdullah Mohammad Sindi,

> of all the religious wars in human history waged by any religion, at any place, and at any time, *none* have been bloodier, more genocidal, more barbaric, and more protracted than the 200-year 'holy wars' by the Western Crusades against the Arabs and Islam. The Western Crusaders horrifically soaked Asia Minor [now Turkey] and the Eastern Arab Mediterranean coast with Arab blood. . . . The objective of the Crusades was simple—to destroy the Arabs . . . in the Holy Land.[48]

That the crusaders attempted to fulfill that terrible goal is not all that surprising, Sindi suggests. After all, he points out, Urban openly called on Christians to go to the Levant and "exterminate this vile race from our lands."[49] By "vile race," of course, he meant Arabs and other Muslims living in that part of the world. He did not urge his followers to expel or push back the Muslims, but rather to "exterminate" them.

That those followers would obligingly agree to carry out that horrendous suggestion says a great deal about the intelligence and morality of those Europeans at the time. Indeed, Sindi says, the Crusades occurred during Western Europe's Dark Age. At that time, he states, Europeans were quite backward compared to the inhabitants of the Muslim world. Even the Christian Byzantines were more culturally advanced than their Western Christian cousins. Thus, Sindi goes on, the crusaders acted against the Muslims even more brutally than they normally did against one another. Their awful

> behavior during their vicious wars reflected their cruelty and primitive barbarism. They were extremely militant, and committed incredible mass violence. They acted like the modern-day violent American Ku Klux Klan and other Western racist groups. They committed, both in Europe and the Arab/Muslim world, the worst conceivable horrible crimes and atrocities, not only against thousands of innocent Muslims and Jews of both sexes and of all ages, but also even against Christians. Their vicious crimes [against] noncombatants and innocent peoples included the destruction of properties; pillaging; plundering; foraging; ravaging; stealing; setting houses on fire; torturing; murdering; executing; burning humans alive; [and] raping women, including nuns.[50]

The Franks Outnumbered

Still another reason that the Christian crusaders fought more brutally than they usually did against one another had to do with their numbers. They felt they had to be more violent than normal because they were badly outnumbered by the enemy. Western historians used to think that hundreds of thousands of Europeans fought in each crusade, or at least in the biggest ones. But twentieth-century research showed this to be incorrect. In reality, their numbers were relatively small, considering how many military operations they engaged in.

> **"[The crusaders] acted like the modern-day violent American Ku Klux Klan and other Western racist groups."[50]**
>
> —Saudi scholar Abdullah Mohammad Sindi

In the First Crusade, for instance, arguably one of the two largest, only about twelve thousand crusaders were stationed in the Levant at any given time. Moreover, only about twelve hundred of them were trained knights, the cream of European fighters. Later, in the Third Crusade, Christian numbers were occasionally higher, but not by much. At the Battle of Hattin, for example, fought in 1187 between a coalition of Christian lords and the Muslim sultan Saladin, the Christians numbered nineteen thousand at most. In contrast, Saladin had at least thirty thousand soldiers.

In order to make up for their inferior numbers, the Christians often committed acts of extreme violence, both on and off the battlefield. This was intended to intimidate the enemy, and it often worked. Gibbon described an instance in which a Frankish soldier literally cut a captive's body in half near a Muslim village. This pitiless act, Gibbon wrote, "taught the [locals] to keep within their walls."[51] The annals of medieval warfare show clearly that acts of this overpoweringly cruel nature rarely took place in European warfare beyond the Crusades.

The Crusades Were Not More Brutal than Other Medieval Wars

"[Medieval warfare] was limited only by the resources of the parties and the technology of the age. The same [level of] brutality prevailed where [very] different societies confronted one another, as on the Crusades."

—Historian John France

John France, *Western Warfare in the Age of the Crusades, 1000–1300*. New York: Cornell University Press, 1999, p. 52.

Consider these questions as you read:

1. On what basis can one war be judged more or less brutal than other wars?
2. Do you think that an organized fighting force is more or less likely to commit brutal acts? Why?
3. How strong is the argument that having a huge army reduces the need for or likelihood of extreme violence being perpetrated on the enemy? Explain your answer.

Editor's note: The discussion that follows presents common arguments made in support of this perspective. All arguments are supported by facts, quotes, and examples taken from various sources of the period or present day.

The war waged in the Holy Land by the crusaders was no different from war waged during other medieval conflicts. It was neither more violent nor more cruel. During the period from about 1000 to 1300, which included most of the Crusades, one military historian states, "there was an unchanging appearance of war."[52] Indeed, the pace of military change, including advances in military technology, was minimal at best in that era. "It would be absurd to suggest that either side enjoyed a technological [advantage]," military historian Christon I. Archer points out. "Technological change, in fact, was minimal during this period and no battle was won due to the clear-cut effect of a superior weapon. At best, both sides endlessly altered old weapons or combinations of the same."[53]

A Kind of Universality of Warfare

This relative absence of military advances extended from Europe into the Middle East so that there was no quantitative difference between the style of fighting in the wars fought in Europe and the Crusades. Furthermore, very few large-scale battles were fought in the medieval period, including the crusading centuries, either in Europe or the Levant. This was mainly because, as remains true today, waging war on a big scale was hugely expensive. All the existing nation-states lacked the money and resources to raise and maintain large armies and take them on extended campaigns, except on rare occasions. "Even when armies of considerable size *were* raised," military historian John France explains, "major engagements were rare. The leaders who gathered armies had to invest enormous resources of their own and to persuade others, many of whom might be doubtful adherents, to do likewise. Weapons, warhorses, means of transport, the paraphernalia [equipment] of war—all of these represented a huge investment of resources."[54]

"Even when armies of considerable size were raised, major engagements were rare."[54]

—Military historian John France

So in both Europe and the Levant, the emphasis in warfare tended to be less on major battles and more on raiding (also called ravaging) and laying siege to castles or walled towns. "The staple of war" in both European-based conflicts and the Crusades, France says, "was the raid—a cheap and expedient way of undermining the economy and willpower of your enemy. Even when a larger force was gathered, its primary function was to destroy, and in so doing feed itself. Ravaging was integral to the business of feeding an army and therefore a central part of war."[55]

All of these factors—the slow pace of technological change, use of the same fighting styles everywhere, the great expense of war, the rarity of large-scale battles, and the emphasis on raids and sieges—ensured a kind of universality of warfare. Whether fought in Europe or in the Middle East, military conflicts tended to look more or less alike. That included the levels of violence and cruelty, which, with occasional exceptions, were more or less the same everywhere.

Lack of Effective Organization

It must also be emphasized that the Crusades were, in most cases, too poorly planned and too disorganized to produce a higher-than-normal level of brutality. For the most part, the soldiers had to focus the bulk of their attention on finding enough food and other supplies to avoid starvation and keep their individual operations going. Cruel acts and atrocities certainly occurred from time to time, as they do in all wars, but there was no concerted policy or overt effort to impose a higher level of brutality than what took place in other conflicts.

"A crusader army was, in effect, a loosely organized mob of soldiers, clergy, servants, and followers."[56]

—Historian Thomas F. Madden

Historian Thomas F. Madden, an expert on the organizational aspects of the Crusades, describes their lack of solid, effective organization like this: "Even crusading kings found it difficult to maintain control over a crusade. Popes in faraway Rome never could. A crusader army was, in effect, a loosely organized mob of soldiers, clergy, servants, and followers heading in roughly the same direction for roughly the same purposes. Once launched, it could be controlled no more than the wind or the sea."[56]

To a large degree this explains why most of the Crusades were failures and why after these wars ended, the Muslims retained control of the Levant for several centuries to come. Some observers disagree. They point to the success of the First Crusade, which, they emphasize, succeeded in wresting Jerusalem from the Turks.

However, that last-minute success actually proves that the crusaders were effective, and capable of focused acts of ruthless brutality, *only* when they were sufficiently organized and coherent as a unified fighting force. As Madden explains, that initial crusade started out as "a long shot" at best. At first, he continues, "there was no leader, no chain of command, no supply lines, no detailed strategy. It was simply thousands of warriors marching deep into enemy territory, committed to a common cause. Many of them died, either in battle or through disease or starvation."[57]

This began to change, however, after the Turks defeated the crusaders in 1097 at Dorylaeum in Anatolia. It was painfully clear to the losers that their defeat stemmed from their having no overall leader with a clear-cut strategy. "Thereafter," France writes, "what had been a relatively incoherent [mass of separate armies] became more coherent and experienced, and more successful."[58] The problem was that this unity of purpose and effective organization was temporary. Most of the operations in the Levant during the later crusades suffered from the same incoherence seen in the First Crusade's early stages. As a result, although isolated acts of extreme brutality by crusaders did happen, they were overall similar to those in all wars—whether ancient, medieval, or modern.

The Normal Rules of War

There was another reason why the Crusades were no more brutal than other wars of their time. It was that most crusaders felt they had no need to be more violent and cruel than normal, because they had plenty of soldiers. In their eyes they had enough to achieve victory without resorting to an outlandish level of brutality. Modern military historians, including John France, hold that the crusader armies were often larger than those typically raised in European military campaigns.

For instance, one of the biggest armies ever assembled in medieval Europe was that of Norman lord William the Conqueror. In 1066 he mobilized some fourteen thousand soldiers for his invasion of Saxon-held England. By modern standards, of course, that number is quite small. But at the time it was seen as an enormous military force.

Much more common were the forces that kings and other powerful medieval lords were able to raise in an emergency. Consider the case of England's king Henry II (reigned 1154–1189). The most fighters he could raise on short notice was six hundred foot soldiers and a few hundred mounted knights. One of Henry's successors, Edward I (1272–1307), was able to do better. In 1287 Edward raised some twenty thousand soldiers to put down

William the Conqueror and his army sailed to England in 1066. William's force of fourteen thousand French troops was quite large for a medieval army, but the First Crusade armies were more than four times that size.

a rebellion. Yet not all of those men fought together at one time in any one battle. At most, a quarter of them could be mustered for a single engagement.

During the Crusades, in contrast, European lords combined their mostly small armies into military forces that were nearly unheard-of back in Europe. Upward of sixty thousand soldiers fought in the First Crusade alone, for example. Somewhere between six thousand and seven thousand of them were knights. That was a huge number of knights for a medieval European force.

A more specific instance is the Battle of Hattin (in what is now Israel), fought in 1187 between Muslim forces and an alliance of Christian leaders. The crusaders had between twelve hundred and fifteen hundred knights. They also had upward of eighteen thousand infantry. In total, that was a far larger force than most European rulers normally raised.

Considering these facts about Christian numbers during the Crusades, the crusaders viewed their forces as more than sufficient in size to achieve a conventional victory. With occasional exceptions, they felt confident enough to follow the normal rules of warfare that they were used to. As France points out, "In general the normal 'rules of engagement' for sieges were accepted on both sides."[59] Moreover, capturing a place or prisoners in battle was largely the same for Muslims in the Levant as for Christians in Europe. Therefore, France adds, these sorts of rules of warfare in the West applied in the Crusades as well. Thus, although now and then acts of brutality occurred, most of the time the crusaders followed the normal rules of medieval warfare.

Chapter Five

Is Seeking Revenge for the Crusades an Inspiration for Modern Islamists?

Seeking Revenge for the Crusades Is an Inspiration for Modern Islamists

- Widely influential modern Muslim writer Sayyid Qutb believed that the Crusades never really ended and that the West was corrupt.
- Motivated by Qutb's writings, al Qaeda attacked the West partly to achieve revenge for the Crusades.
- ISIS's members also view Americans and other Westerners as modern-day crusaders.

Seeking Revenge for the Crusades Does Not Motivate Modern Islamists

- By the early 1800s most Muslims had largely forgotten about the Crusades, an overall victory from their remote past.
- The idea of the Crusades as a Western attack on Islam was an artificial construct created in the mid-1800s by an opinionated French historian.
- Modern Islamist terrorists only use the Crusades as an excuse for their attempts to extend their own views and rule around the world.

Seeking Revenge for the Crusades Is an Inspiration for Modern Islamists

"In the First Crusade, when the Christian soldiers took Jerusalem they [killed] every woman and child who was Muslim. [I] can tell you that that story is still being told today in the Middle East and we are still paying for it."

Forty-second US president Bill Clinton

Quoted in Thomas Madden, "Rivers of Blood: An Analysis of One Aspect of the Crusader Conquest of Jerusalem in 1099," Medievalists.net, October 6, 2013. www.medievalists.net.

Consider these questions as you read:

1. Why do you think the Crusades continue to fuel hatred for the West among extreme Islamist groups?
2. In your opinion, what did Egyptian writer Sayyid Qutb get wrong and get right in his writings about American culture?
3. Can you think of any other events in recent times that might have been influenced or inspired by events from long ago? Explain.

Editor's note: The discussion that follows presents common arguments made in support of this perspective. All arguments are supported by facts, quotes, and examples taken from various sources of the period or present day.

One of the central beliefs of the influential twentieth-century Egyptian writer and educator Sayyid Qutb was that the Crusades never really ended. Qutb, who died in 1966, argued that the powers that long ago sought to eradicate Muslims from the Holy Land have been succeeded by others who are equally intent on destroying Islam. Qutb's views have inspired modern Islamists, who see their violent actions as a form of vengeance for the attacks of the crusaders on Muslims in the Middle East some eight centuries ago.

America Immoral and Soulless?

Qutb's hatred for the West was already partly formed when he moved to Greeley, Colorado, in 1949 to study at the local school that later became the University of Northern Colorado. His glimpses of modern American life shocked and angered him. He thereafter condemned American culture as uncouth, immoral, and soulless. The United States was no place for decent Muslims to live, he concluded.

Qutb's subsequent writings, which would eventually inspire numerous radical Islamist organizations, criticized both America and other Western countries. He viewed them as degenerate and still harboring the crusading spirit. Qutb wrote:

> This great America: What is its worth in the scale of human values? And what does it add to the moral account of humanity? And, by the journey's end, what will its contribution be? I fear that a balance may not exist between America's material greatness and the quality of its people. And I fear that the wheel of life will have turned [and] America will have added nothing, or next to nothing, to the account of morals that distinguishes man from object, and indeed, mankind from animals.[60]

To show his Muslim readers that American men were no different than the brutal crusaders, Qutb singled out the American game of football. He saw it as a primitive, mindless metaphor for the imperialistic crusaders. "It seems the American is primitive in his appreciation of muscular strength," he stated. American men have no values, principles, or manners in their personal and family lives, he went on. "This primitiveness can be seen in the spectacle of the fans as they follow a game of football." Each player, Qutb wrote, tries

> to catch the ball with his hands and run with it toward the goal, while the players of the opposing team attempt to tackle him by any means necessary, whether this be a blow

> to his stomach, or crushing his arms and legs with great violence and ferocity. The sight of the fans as they follow this game, or watch boxing matches or bloody, monstrous wrestling matches [reveals] animal excitement born of their love for hardcore violence. [They] are enthralled with the flowing blood and crushed limbs. [Destroy] his head. Crush his ribs. Beat him to a pulp. This spectacle leaves no room for doubt as to the primitiveness of the feelings of those who are enamored with muscular strength.[61]

In Qutb's narrow-minded and somewhat paranoid outlook, America and other Western countries posed a serious danger to the world. They blinded decent people to the "true" civilization that the Prophet Muhammad had begun in the seventh century. The modern world had regressed to the barbarous state it had been in *before* Muhammad, Qutb theorized. Much of the fault belonged to the violent crusaders and the equally corrupt Jews. The only remedy, he said, was for all true Muslims to save human civilization through jihad, or holy war, against the West.

> **"It seems the American is primitive in his appreciation of muscular strength."[61]**
>
> —Egyptian writer and educator Sayyid Qutb

Ingrained in Muslim Hearts and Minds

Qutb's extreme views were rejected by most Muslims—and in fact, the Egyptian government labeled him a troublemaker and executed him in 1966. But his writings lived on and over time influenced new generations of Islamist extremists. Indeed, captivated by those writings, the terrorist group al Qaeda plotted its deadly attacks on the West, partly to get revenge on Westerners for the supposed outrages of the Crusades.

Yet extremists were not the only Muslims who at least agreed with Qutb in principle. That is, some concurred that the modern

Those who orchestrated the attacks on the World Trade Center in 2001 spoke of resisting another Western crusade in the Middle East. Since then, other violent Muslim groups have proposed building an Islamic caliphate to reclaim the region and cast out Western interests and aggressors.

West was an extension of the crusader nations of old and posed a threat to Islam, although they did not agree that violence was the way to fix the situation. Some Muslim intellectuals still feel this way, and their writings provide a fascinating window into the mind of Qutb and the extremists who *do* advocate violence against the West. Consider the words of the nonviolent Saudi scholar Abdullah Mohammad Sindi. "As a result of the centuries of Western conflicts and contacts with the Arabs," he writes,

> the age of the greedy Western international capitalism and brutal colonialism/imperialism has emerged. [It exists] to

> the detriment and misery of the native peoples of North America, Central America, South America, the Caribbean, [Asia], Africa, and the Arab world. Hence, the most important legacy of the crusaders has been the sanctification [approval] of Western violence against non-Europeans in pursuit of imperialist and capitalist ends.[62]

The underlying concept of crusading against Muslims, Sindi contends, has been absorbed into Western culture. When the Crusades physically ended, he claims, Europeans kept the spirit of those wars alive in their political and economic structures. As a result, Western democracy has come to replace the Catholic Church as a sacred cause to justify aggression against Islam.

"Arab hatred for the West, because of the Crusades, has been painfully re-ignited by the vicious Western colonization and dismemberment of the Arab nation during the 19th and 20th centuries."[63]

—Saudi scholar Abdullah Mohammad Sindi

In this way, Sindi echoes Qutb when he says that the original hostilities between Muslims and the West

> are still lingering on. The Crusaders' gory massacres and barbaric cannibalism in the Arab world created a great deal of hate for the imperialist West which has since been ingrained in the hearts and minds of most Arabs and Muslims. And since the 19th century new waves of Western aggression and wars against the Arabs have been taking place. Arab hatred for the West, because of the Crusades, has been painfully re-ignited by the vicious Western colonization and dismemberment of the Arab nation during the 19th and 20th centuries.[63]

Sindi and others like him seek to identify the causes of the continuing breach between the West and Islam. A few Islamist extremists have taken this information and rhetoric a step further, into the realm of violence and mass murder. The former leader of al Qaeda, Osama bin Laden, was perhaps the most widely publicized of those individuals. On September 11, 2001, which thereafter became emblazoned in the historical annals as 9/11, his henchmen attacked the United States using airliners as weapons.

At first, many Americans and other Westerners were perplexed about why al Qaeda would perpetrate such awful butchery against fellow humans. But the motive became crystal clear in March 2003. In a statement to the world, Bin Laden said, "The Zionist [Jewish]-Crusader campaign [against Islam] today is the most dangerous and rabid ever." To learn "how to resist these enemy forces from outside," he continued, "we must look at the previous Crusader wars against our [Muslim] countries."[64]

A Final Crusade?

Although Bin Laden paid the price for his crimes when US Navy SEALs killed him in 2011, al Qaeda lives on. Furthermore, other Islamist extremists have declared war on the West in part for its role in the Crusades. It is difficult to decide which of these groups is the most insidious and barbarous. But ISIS (also called ISIL) may well hold that dubious honor. Technically known as the Islamic State in Iraq and the Levant, it seeks to achieve revenge for the Crusades. But unlike al Qaeda, ISIS desires to create a caliphate, or Islamic empire, which its members hope will eventually conquer the entire world. ISIS's first attempt to build its caliphate, centered in Iraq and northern Syria, failed. These areas were liberated from that group's control between 2015 and 2017 by Iraqi and other forces, aided by the United States and its allies. However, core members of ISIS remain dangerous and hope to conquer more territory when the opportunity arises.

Moreover, ISIS's leaders believe that the West will launch an apocalyptic final crusade and that its armies will meet those of

Islam near the Syrian town of Dabiq. There, supposedly, ISIS will be triumphant. In a 2014 ISIS propaganda video, a masked executioner beheaded a Western captive, Peter Kassig. "Here we are," the narrator droned, "burying the first American crusader in Dabiq, eagerly waiting for the remainder of your armies to arrive."[65]

The use of crusader terminology and other references to the Crusades shows clearly that those medieval conflicts were far reaching in their effects. For many Islamist extremists, those wars are still, in a very real sense, ongoing. The bitterest of these terrorists say they will not be satisfied until the West endures the utter destruction they feel it deserves.

Seeking Revenge for the Crusades Does Not Motivate Modern Islamists

"[The Crusades] evoke a romantic image of medieval knights, chivalry, romance, and religious high-mindedness. But representing them as wars between Christians and Muslims is a gross oversimplification and a misreading of history."

—University of Sydney scholar Carol Cusack

Carol Cusack, "Did the Crusades Lead to Islamic State?," The Conversation. https://theconversation.com.

Consider these questions as you read:

1. What do you think about the idea that Muslims were the actual victors in the years-long wars known as the Crusades? Explain your answer.
2. How do the words of prominent people shape attitudes toward events of the past and present, and how can individuals identify truth from falsehood or exaggeration?
3. How were the Crusades of the medieval era turned into a rationale for actions in the modern age?

Editor's note: The discussion that follows presents common arguments made in support of this perspective. All arguments are supported by facts, quotes, and examples taken from various sources of the period or present day.

The notion that modern Islamists seek to get revenge on Christians for the way Muslims were treated during the Crusades is false. First, looking back on the crusading era as a whole, the Muslims *won* those so-called holy wars. The European Christians who instigated the Crusades were eventually driven away from the Levant in utter humiliation. Not only did the Muslims recapture Jerusalem and its environs, they also defeated and eradicated the crusader enclaves making up the Outremer. Thus, if anyone involved in those conflicts had reason to hold bitter memories and the hope of someday achieving revenge, it would be the Christians, *not* the Muslims.

Conflicts from a Bygone Age

Moreover, the supposed bitter memories, said by some to constitute a direct link between the Muslims of the crusader era and modern Muslims, simply never existed until the nineteenth century. The reality is that by the early 1800s, most Muslims had largely forgotten about the Crusades. What is more, the few who did recall them correctly viewed them as an overall Muslim victory from the remote past. For the vast majority of Muslims, historian Christopher Tyerman states, after the fifteenth century, the memory of the Crusades "slipped into the quiet reaches of history."[66] Another noted expert on the Crusades, Thomas Asbridge, expands a bit on that point. In the nineteenth century, he writes, "Islam exhibited very little interest in the Crusades. [At the time] most Muslims seem to have regarded the war for the Holy Land as a largely irrelevant conflict, fought in a bygone age. True, the barbarous Franks had invaded the Levant and carried out acts of violence, but they had been roundly punished and defeated. Islam had, quite naturally, prevailed."[67]

Still more proof for the lack of Islamic worry or anger over the Crusades takes the form of a revealing excerpt from one of the letters of T.E. Lawrence. Better known as Lawrence of Arabia, he was a famous Englishman who befriended and fought alongside Arabs in the Middle East during World War I. In the letter, Lawrence described an event he personally witnessed—the post–World War I negotiation between French leader Stephen Pichon and Arab chieftain Faisal al-Hashemi. Desiring to possess a chunk of Syria, Pichon told Faisal that French interest in that region went all the way back to the Crusades. In response, the

"But, pardon me, which of us won the Crusades?"[68]

—Arab chieftain Faisal al-Hashemi to a French leader

quick-witted Faisal said (according to Lawrence), "But, pardon me, which of us won the Crusades?"[68]

Faisal's remark was generally representative of the Muslim attitude toward the Crusades before World War I. To him, those wars represented a long-ago Muslim victory over the West and therefore were nothing that modern Europeans should dredge up and waste time on in the present. In fact, California University of Pennsylvania scholar Paul Crawford points out, "Most of the Arabic-language historical writing on the Crusades before the mid-nineteenth century was produced by Arab Christians, not Muslims, and most of that was positive."[69] That is, in the late 1800s and early 1900s only Christians were still fixed on the memory of the Crusades, while most Muslims barely remembered those conflicts and cared little about them.

To Rid the World of Inferiors?

In a like manner, the very idea of the Crusades as a Western attack on Islam did not originate with Muslims who remembered those conflicts and were angry about them. Rather, that concept was an artificial construct created in the early 1800s by an opinionated French historian named Joseph-François Michaud. During that period there were two principal European schools of thought concerning the Crusades. One, promoted by great writers like France's Voltaire and Britain's Edward Gibbon and Walter Scott, viewed the crusaders as greedy, violent barbarians who assaulted civilized, peace-loving Muslims in the Levant.

The other school of thought regarding the Crusades, which was more romantic, was championed by some initially lesser-known writers, including Michaud. They viewed those medieval wars, Crawford says, "as a glorious episode in a long-standing struggle in which Christian chivalry had driven back Muslim hordes."[70] Michaud published his massive *History of the Crusades* in 1822. It proved to be extremely popular and in many ways reshaped public views about the Crusades among the French, British, Americans, and other Westerners. In his highly romanticized and idealistic version of those past conflicts, the crusaders were heroes of the highest stature who fought to rid the world of so-called inferiors. Indeed, Michaud came right out and said that the Franks, like the Europeans of his own day, were superior to other peoples, including Muslims. The crusaders, he insisted, were honorable, chivalrous, virtuous, religiously devout, and exceptionally civilized.

In marked contrast, Michaud viewed Islam as a threat to the West. In his eyes, it was an ongoing danger that was both menacing and barbaric. This harsh criticism of Islam inspired positive reactions from many Westerners and negative ones from numerous Muslims. According to Tyerman, Michaud's "portrait of crusading as mortal combat with a degraded, almost demonized Islam, [when] translated into Arabic produced [serious] consequences still being played out in modern political conflicts."[71]

Despite its controversial and influential nature, Michaud's presentation of the Crusades had, and still has, little connection with reality, as numerous respected modern historians point out. Thomas Asbridge explains that in Michaud's work "the political, cultural, and spiritual resonances of the distant Crusades have been manufactured by an imaginary view of the past."[72]

Tyerman agrees but concedes that Michaud's distorted vision of Western Christians putting lowly medieval Muslims in their place was powerful. Modern Muslims were sure to be offended by it. Thus, Michaud's history of the Crusades provided the fuel for equally imprecise interpretations of the Crusades that appeared in the twentieth century. "The idea of the Crusades as explicit precursors to modern events," Tyerman says, "remains potent." Even in the early twenty-first century, people on both sides of the issue are drawn to Michaud's false thesis in part because it contains a vivid, compelling "combination of ideology, action, change, European conquest, and religious fanaticism,"[73] according to Tyerman.

Their Own Twisted Goals

Sayyid Qutb, Osama bin Laden, and other Islamist extremists were well aware that the crusade-themed rhetoric of Michaud and other similarly misguided Western writers upset many Muslims. It is not surprising, therefore, that Bin Laden and other fanatics used the Crusades as an excuse for bad behavior. They hoped to get as many Muslims as they could to back their violent acts against the West.

> **"The idea of the Crusades as explicit precursors to modern events remains potent."[73]**
>
> **—Historian Christopher Tyerman**

So individuals like Bin Laden often cited European aggression in those long-ago wars to justify fulfilling their own twisted goals around the globe. Their real motivations for committing mass murder and other crimes against Western peoples are *not* the Crusades. Instead, they are overblown religious zeal and a naked desire to hold power over others. In Crawford's words, early twentieth-century Islamist extremists "borrowed the idea of a long-standing European campaign against them from the former European school of thought [exemplified by Michaud's ideas], missing the fact that this was a serious [misrepresentation] of the Crusades and using this distorted understanding as a way to generate support for their own agendas."[74]

In the late twentieth century, a new generation of Islamist bad actors, including Bin Laden, concluded that they could fight the West and win and therefore initiated large-scale terrorist acts. Most Muslims did not agree that such violence was either right or fruitful. But a small but vocal minority of Muslims, historian Jonathan Riley-Smith says, were receptive to this extremist message. They were already undergoing "a worldwide revival of what was then called Islamic fundamentalism and is now sometimes referred to, a bit clumsily, as jihadism."[75]

Until his dying day, Bin Laden continued to use the Crusades as a justification for his and his followers' murderous acts. Most of the support he maintained among Muslims still came from those who had no real concept of what actually happened in the Crusades. They believed Bin Laden's distortions. The history he fed them was "a feverish fantasy," Crawford explains. He was

The leaders of ISIS claim a desire to establish an autonomous Islamic state. In 2014 the group launched a war in Syria and Iraq to begin building its caliphate.

"no more accurate in his view about the Crusades than he [was] about the supposed perfect Islamic unity which he [imagined] Islam enjoyed before the baleful influence of Christianity intruded."[76]

Asbridge ably sums up what more educated Muslims and Christians alike know to be true:

> The notion that the struggle for domination of the Holy Land so many centuries ago does, or somehow should, have a direct bearing on the modern world is misguided. The reality of these medieval wars must be explored and understood if the forces of propaganda are to be [diminished]. And incitements to hostility [must be] countered. But the Crusades must also be placed where they belong: in the past.[77]

Source Notes

Chapter One: A Brief History of the Crusades

1. Christopher Tyerman, *The Crusades: A Very Short Introduction*. New York: Oxford University Press, 2005, pp. iii–iv.
2. Quoted in Medieval Sourcebook, "Urban II's Speech at Council of Clermont, 1095, Five Versions of the Speech," Fordham University, 1997. https://sourcebooks.fordham.edu.
3. Thomas F. Madden, *The Concise History of the Crusades*. Lanham, MD: Rowman and Littlefield, 2013, p. 18.
4. Quoted in Medieval Sourcebook, "Peter the Hermit and the Popular Crusade, Collected Accounts," Fordham University, 1997. https://sourcebooks.fordham.edu.
5. Quoted in Medieval Sourcebook, "The Siege and Capture of Jerusalem, Collected Accounts," Fordham University, 1997. https://sourcebooks.fordham.edu.
6. Thomas Asbridge, *The Crusades*. New York: HarperCollins, 2010, p. 658.
7. Quoted in Francesco Gabrieli, *Arab Historians of the Crusades*. New York: Barnes and Noble, 1993, p. 346.

Chapter Two: Was Retaking the Holy Land the Purpose of the First Crusade?

8. Quoted in Medieval Sourcebook, "Urban II's Speech at Council of Clermont, 1095, Five Versions of the Speech."
9. Quoted in August C. Krey, ed., *The First Crusade: The Accounts of Eyewitnesses and Participants*. Charleston, SC: Nabu, 2014, p. 33.
10. Quran 9:30–31.
11. Efraim Karsh, *Islamic Imperialism: A History*. New Haven, CT: Yale University Press, 2006, pp. 22–23.
12. Asbridge, *The Crusades*, p. 35.
13. Asbridge, *The Crusades*, p. 36.
14. Karen Armstrong, *Holy War: The Crusades and Their Impact on Today's World*. New York: Random House, 2001, p. xii.
15. Madden, *The Concise History of the Crusades*, p. 11.

16. Quoted in J.J. Saunders, *Aspects of the Crusades*. Christchurch, New Zealand: University of Canterbury Press, 1962, pp. 11–12.
17. Edward Gibbon, *The Decline and Fall of the Roman Empire*, vol. 3, ed. David Womersley. New York: Penguin, 1994, p. 568.
18. Quoted in Medieval Sourcebook, "Urban II's Speech at Council of Clermont, 1095, Five Versions of the Speech."
19. Quoted in Krey, *The First Crusade*, p. 34.
20. Quran 109.
21. Steven Runciman, *A History of the Crusades, vol. 1, The First Crusade and the Foundation of the Kingdom of Jerusalem*. New York: Penguin, 2016, p. 37.

Chapter Three: Did the Crusaders Commit Atrocities?

22. Quoted in Medieval Sourcebook, "Albert of Aix and Ekkehard of Aura: Emico and the Slaughter of the Rhineland Jews," Fordham University, 1997. https://sourcebooks.fordham.edu.
23. Quoted in Medieval Sourcebook, "Albert of Aix and Ekkehard of Aura."
24. Quoted in Medieval Sourcebook, "Albert of Aix and Ekkehard of Aura."
25. Guibert of Nogent, *The Deeds of God Through the Franks*. Rochester, NY: Boydell, 1997, p. 132.
26. Quoted in Krey, *The First Crusade*, p. 261.
27. Guibert of Nogent, *The Deeds of God Through the Franks*, p. 132.
28. Quoted in Edward Peters, ed., *The First Crusade: The Chronicle of Fulcher of Chartres and Other Source Materials*. Philadelphia: University of Pennsylvania Press, 1998, p. 91.
29. Quoted in Peters, *The First Crusade*, p. 84.
30. Quoted in Asbridge, *The Crusades*, p. 85.
31. Quoted in Peters, *The First Crusade*, pp. 84–85.
32. Rodney Stark, *God's Battalions: The Case for the Crusades*. New York: HarperCollins, 2009, pp. 157–58.
33. John France, "Impelled by the Love of God," in *Crusades: The Illustrated History*, ed. Thomas F. Madden. Ann Arbor: University of Michigan Press, 2007, p. 47.
34. Asbridge, *The Crusades*, p. 102.
35. France, "Impelled by the Love of God," p. 47.

36. Madden, *The Concise History of the Crusades*, p. 20.
37. Leon Poliakov, *The History of Anti-Semitism: From the Time of Christ to the Court Jews*, vol. 1. New York: Vanguard, 1965, p. 45.
38. Runciman, *A History of the Crusades,* vol. 1, p. 141.
39. Usama ibn Munqidh, *The Book of Contemplation*, trans. Paul M. Cobb. New York: Penguin, 2008, p. 25.
40. Ibn Munqidh, *The Book of Contemplation*, p. 81.
41. Ibn Munqidh, *The Book of Contemplation*, p. 81.

Chapter Four: Were the Crusades More Brutal than Other Medieval Wars?

42. G.W. Foote and J.M. Wheeler, *Crimes of Christianity*. London: Progressive, 1887, p. 179.
43. Foote and Wheeler, *Crimes of Christianity*, p. 178.
44. Gibbon, *The Decline and Fall of the Roman Empire*, vol. 3, p. 565.
45. Runciman, *A History of the Crusades,* vol. 1, p. 92.
46. Runciman, *A History of the Crusades,* vol. 1, p. 92.
47. Foote and Wheeler, *Crimes of Christianity*, p. 201.
48. Abdullah Mohammad Sindi, "The Western Christian Terrorism Against the Arabs: The Cannibalism and Bloodbaths of the Crusades, 1095–1291." Radio Islam. https://radioislam.org.
49. Quoted in Sindi, "The Western Christian Terrorism Against the Arabs."
50. Sindi, "The Western Christian Terrorism Against the Arabs."
51. Gibbon, *The Decline and Fall of the Roman Empire*, vol. 3, pp. 594–95.
52. John France, *Western Warfare in the Age of the Crusades, 1000–1300*. New York: Cornell University Press, 1999, p. 16.
53. Christon I. Archer et al., *World History of Warfare*. Lincoln: University of Nebraska Press, 2008, pp. 164–65.
54. France, *Western Warfare in the Age of the Crusades, 1000–1300*, p. 8.
55. France, *Western Warfare in the Age of the Crusades, 1000–1300*, p. 12.
56. Madden, *The Concise History of the Crusades*, p. 10.
57. Thomas F. Madden, "The Real History of the Crusades," *Crisis*, April 1, 2002. www.crisismagazine.com.

58. John France, *Victory in the East: A Military History of the First Crusade*. New York: Cambridge University Press, 1994, p. 371.
59. France, *Western Warfare in the Age of the Crusades, 1000–1300*, p. 228.

Chapter Five: Is Seeking Revenge for the Crusades an Inspiration for Modern Islamists?

60. Sayyid Qutb, "The America I Have Seen," Internet Archive. https://archive.org.
61. Qutb, "The America I Have Seen."
62. Sindi, "The Western Christian Terrorism Against the Arabs."
63. Sindi, "The Western Christian Terrorism Against the Arabs."
64. Quoted in Umej Bhatia, *Forgetting Osama bin Munqidh, Remembering Osama bin Laden: The Crusades in Modern Muslim Memory*. Singapore: S. Rajaratnum School of International Studies, 2008, pp. 52–53.
65. Quoted in BBC, "Dabiq: Why Is That Syrian Town So Important for ISIS?," October 4, 2016. www.bbc.com.
66. Tyerman, *The Crusades*, p. 137.
67. Asbridge, *The Crusades*, pp. 670–71.
68. Quoted in Robert Graves and B.H. Liddell Hart, *T.E. Lawrence to His Biographers*. Garden City, NY: Doubleday, 1938, p. 52.
69. Paul Crawford, "Four Myths About the Crusades," Catholic Education Resource Center, 2011. www.catholiceducation.org.
70. Crawford, "Four Myths About the Crusades."
71. Tyerman, *The Crusades*, p. 109.
72. Asbridge, *The Crusades*, p. 680.
73. Tyerman, *The Crusades*, p. 121.
74. Crawford, "Four Myths About the Crusades."
75. Jonathan Riley-Smith, *The Crusades, Christianity, and Islam*. New York: Columbia University Press, 2008, p. 73.
76. Crawford, "Four Myths About the Crusades."
77. Asbridge, *The Crusades*, p. 681.

For Further Research

Books

Andrew Coddington, *Strategic Inventions of the Crusades*. New York: Cavendish Square, 2017.

Angus Konstam, *Byzantine Warship vs. Arab Warship: 7th–11th Centuries*. London: Osprey, 2015.

David Nicolle, *Crusader Castles in the Holy Land, 1192–1302*. London: Osprey, 2005.

David Nicolle, *The First Crusade, 1096–99: Conquest of the Holy Land*. London: Osprey, 2003.

David Nicolle, *The Second Crusade, 1148: Disaster Outside Damascus*. London: Osprey, 2009.

David Nicolle, *The Third Crusade, 1191: Richard the Lionheart, Saladin, and the Struggle for Jerusalem*. London: Osprey, 2005.

Edith Wilmot-Buxtun, *The Story of the Crusades*. Charleston, SC: Amazon Digital, 2017.

Internet Sources

As'ad AbuKhalil, "The Legacy of the Crusades in the Contemporary Muslim World," Al Jazeera, December 28, 2016. www.aljazeera.com/indepth/opinion/2016/12/legacy-crusades-contemporary-muslim-world-161224124349711.html.

Catholic Encyclopedia, "Peter the Hermit," 2017. www.newadvent.org/cathen/11775b.htm.

History, "1095: Pope Urban II Orders the First Crusade," 2018. www.history.com/topics/crusades.

Al Jazeera, "Liberation: Acre and the End of the Crusades," December 28, 2016. www.aljazeera.com/programmes/the-crusades-an-arab-perspective/2016/12/liberation-fall-acre-crusades-161225103519869.html.

Medieval Sourcebook, "Richard the Lionheart Makes Peace with Saladin, 1192," Fordham University, 1997. https://sourcebooks.fordham.edu/source/1192peace.asp.

York University, "Richard of Holy Trinity," (medieval manuscript about the Third Crusade), 2001. www.yorku.ca/inpar/richard_of_holy_trinity.pdf.

Websites

Crusades, *Catholic Encyclopedia* (www.newadvent.org/cathen/04543c.htm#I). This highly informative site contains more than a hundred links to other websites containing data on European and Muslim leaders, cities, fortresses, battles, peoples, religious terms, and much more.

The Crusades, History (www.history.com/topics/crusades). This site gives a useful general historical overview of the Crusades, explaining why each one was fought and the results of the fighting. Links to other web pages provide extra information about places, leaders, and battles.

Timeline for the Crusades and Christian Holy War to c. 1350 (www.usna.edu/Users/history/abels/hh315/crusades_timeline.htm). Compiled by Richard Abels of the US Naval Academy, this expanded chronology contains loads of factual information, along with links to other web pages containing useful information.

Index

Picture Credits

Cover: Duncan1890/iStockphoto.com

6: Shutterstock.com/Sean Pavone (top); Shutterstock.com/jorisvo (bottom)

7: Shutterstock.com/vkilikov (top left); iStockphoto.com/sedmak (top right); Shutterstock.com/LizCoughhlan

11: Maury Aaseng

19: Taking of Jerusalem by the Crusaders, 15th July 1099, 1847 (oil on canvas), Signol, Emile (1804–92)/Château de Versailles, France/Bridgeman Images

24: Pope Urban II announcing First Crusade, 1095, miniature taken from This history of Crusades by Guillaume de Tyr, 15th century French manuscript, History of Crusades, 11th century/De Agostini Picture Library/Bridgeman Images

31: Peter the Hermit, Embleton, Gerry (b.1941)/Private Collection/© Look and Learn/Bridgeman Images

38: Fr.20124 f.331 The Looting of Jerusalem after the Capture by the Christians in 1099, illuminated miniature from a universal chronicle, 1440 (vellum), Jean de Courcy, (15th century)/Bibliotheque Nationale, Paris, France/Bridgeman Images

44: Pope Urban II (1040–1099 pope in 1088–1099) chairing the Ecumenical council of Clermont and preaching the crusade, November 27, 1095, detail from 15th century manuscript by Sebastien Mamerot (1490)/PVDE/Bridgeman Images

52: William the Conqueror on his way to conquer England, 1066 (chromolitho), French School, (19th century)/Private Collection/© Look and Learn/Bridgeman Images

58: Associated Press

67: Welayat Raqqa/Zuma Press/Newscom

About the Author

Historian and award-winning author Don Nardo has written numerous books for young adults about the medieval era. These include volumes on medieval warfare, knights and chivalry, castles, the Inquisition, religious pilgrimages, the Vikings, the Black Death, the King Arthur legends, and more. Nardo, who also composes and arranges orchestral music, lives with his wife, Christine, in Massachusetts.